# *Letters to Corey*

©2023 Ellen Bennett

Cojinito Press LLC

This is a work of fiction. All characters, locales, and events are either products of the author's imagination or are used fictitiously.

LETTERS TO COREY   A Novel

Copyright © 2023 by Ellen Bennett.

All rights reserved. No part of this book may be reproduced in any manner whatsoever without written permission from the publisher, save for brief quotations used in critical articles or reviews.

Cover design by Ann McMan

Published by Cojinito Press, LLC

ISBN: 978-0-9980277-5-3

First Edition 2023

Printed in the United States of America

Author photograph: T Reuss

Ellen Bennett

## **Early Feedback for *Letters to Corey:***

Thought provoking and emotional. An amazing read for everyone! Thank you, Ellen, for writing such a wonderful story. - BV

The dialogue and journal entries drive this story. Don't miss a word! - DN

This was an emotional rollercoaster. I could feel every heartbreak and the tears flowed with every page. - KJV

What amazes me is that Ellen has never had children, yet she captures the bottomless love between mother and child as if this story happened to her. Brava! - MB

Five stars! Will make this our next book club read! - Ann

This is an unusual story about how grief and loss can lead to self-discovery. I thoroughly enjoyed it. Bravo, well done! - KDB

Letters to Corey

# PROLOGUE/ PRESENT

*Massachusetts General Hospital, Boston*
*Oncology Unit*
*Sunday October 4, 1981*

All the sounds are normal. Hushed voices from the hallway, a ringing phone at the nurse's station, the squeak of wheels as carts are quietly pushed by his door, the gentle beeping of machines that surround him, his guttural and labored breathing.

She closes her eyes. A steady thrum courses through her temples from her chest. She wonders about the heart's job. If it is as simple as pumping blood through the body, how can it be capable of such immeasurable pain?

Risa sits on the edge of Corey's bed. The dark brown lesions on the exposed parts of his body—in contrast with the pallor of his skin and bald head—give him the appearance of a sickly old man.

He drifts in and out of consciousness.

Deep sadness lodges in the pit of her throat. She knows Corey is nearing the end. All that could have been done was done: the endless tests, the chemo, the newer untested drugs for the virus, the prayers, and good wishes.

Now it is just a morphine-induced haze.

She whispers, "Honey, can you hear me?"

His breathing catches then he attempts to open his eyes. "Mom." His voice, barely a whisper.

Tears form around her forced smile. "I'm right here."

She reaches for his bony hand. He responds by feebly wrapping his fingers around hers. "Will you stay?" It comes out muffled, echoing off the plastic walls of his oxygen mask.

She nods, afraid she will start bawling. Instead, she gently holds his fragile hand. "You were only four months old when I—"

His parched lips break into a minimal smile. "I know." He tries to squeeze her hand but instead grimaces in pain.

She slips her free hand underneath his. "There, how is that?"

He nods, his eyelids slowly drop.

She must look away, at anything that could distract the growing desire to howl. But everything she settles her gaze on reminds her of exactly where she is and why. She thinks about the next patient who will occupy the room. Will that family overcompensate as well? Will they try to instill a sense of normalcy despite the illness? Will they hope their ministrations will be successful enough to bring the patient back from an incurable disease?

Risa looks back down at her son's hand in hers. Tears drop onto their interlaced fingers. She goes to brush them away—like she did so many years ago—but instead leaves the salty liquid from her body to remain on his—a dash of hope that perhaps the absorption might keep him alive for another hour, another day.

Corey slips back into the haze. His breathing becomes more labored, his diaphragm barely able to push damaged lungs. Risa watches his abdomen.

The door opens quietly as Saul steps in. He approaches the bed, kisses Risa, then asks, "Any changes?"

She shakes her head. What she wants to say is *"He's dying, Saul. What changes might miraculously occur?"* But her attention never leaves Corey's chest and for a moment, it does not move.

She leans in sharply, "No! Don't! Oh God, no!"

When his chest finally moves again, it is deep and big, filling his lungs with a solid intake of air. He blows it out with a gurgle, mucus slipping from his lips into the mask. His body tenses, rises slightly, then settles.

Alarms go off immediately.

She looks at the clock over his bed.

Ten thirty-one.

Corey Joseph Shapiro is dead at the age of nineteen from a disease that the medical community will not get a handle on for a long, long time.

Risa collapses over her son's legs.

Ellen Bennett

*This story is dedicated to those who have loved and lost, to the mothers, fathers, sisters, and brothers. To those who fought on the front lines as nurses, doctors, researchers, and clergy.*

*This story is for you.*

Letters to Corey

*Family is not an important thing.
It's everything.*
-Michael J. Fox

Letters to Corey

# CHAPTER ONE

*Manchester, Massachusetts*
*June 1980*

Risa found Corey on the back patio in a lounge chair.
"Mind if I join you?"
"Oh, no, of course not, mom! I thought you and dad went to bed."
She pulled over another lounger to be next to him and settled in. "What a gorgeous sky. Not a cloud around. Look at that moon, lighting up the night."
"It is." He mused, "Remember how we used to count stars then we'd lose track and have to start over again?"
Risa chuckled. "An exercise in futility. But you loved the game, and it made you tired. It was my sure-cure way of getting you to go to bed!"
Corey countered, "Well as I recall, we tried it just a few years ago and *you* dozed off after the third go around!"
Risa crossed her long legs at the ankle and reached for Corey's hand. He interlaced his fingers with hers. She asked, "Are you nervous about school?"
"Mom, I have the whole summer to *not* think about it, but" he hesitated, "it's going to be pretty crazy at first, getting used to the city life and the dorm. So different from Boston. Boston closes early. New York never sleeps!"
Risa hummed the tune, "New York New York…"
"Yeah, maybe I'm a *little* nervous."
"There's going to be so much to take in. The city has a lot to offer and can be overwhelming at times. Knowing you, you'll be out scouting the town before your bags are unpacked. But don't forget why you're there. And you *know* your father is going to be watching your grades like a hawk."
Corey ran his free hand over his face. "Don't I know it."
"He just wants to see you use those fabulous brain cells he claims to be the sole donor of."

Corey barked out a laugh. "You two. You're both a pretty good mix of creative and brains. Rachel is dad, I am you. What could be better?"

"Rachel is truly the pragmatic one. You, you're the one who can charm his way into anything and anyone." She studied his profile—as she often did— in the semi-darkness. He was truly handsome with his mop of wavy jet-black hair, thick dark eyebrows over piercing green eyes, and a long sleek nose. But it was his broad smile that melted her heart.

The joke around the house was; when Corey smiled, everyone smiled, even the constantly crabby.

Corey yawned. "Boy, I'm getting a little sleepy! You?"

Risa sat up and squeezed his hand then let it go. "I think it's time for me to go spoon with that sharp attorney upstairs."

Corey groaned. "Too much information."

Risa stood, leaned down and kissed her son on his head. "Goodnight, honey. See you in the morning."

"Goodnight mom."

\*\*\*

As soon as Corey watched her turn off the kitchen light and disappear down the hallway toward the steps, he got up quickly and walked steadily toward the woods behind the house.

A harsh whisper came from his left. "CJ, over here!"

Corey let his eyes adjust to the dark then strode toward the voice.

"I've been waiting for almost half an hour. I was getting ready to leave."

Corey approached, "I'm sorry. My mom came out and sat with me for a while." He reached out and found a hand, "I'm glad you waited for me."

"I had to see you."

Corey pulled him in, kissing him hard on the mouth. "I'll make it worth your while."

Risa was at the top of the steps when she realized she forgot to ask Corey about the car in the morning. He said he would take it to the shop for an oil change, but she was pretty sure he forgot.

She went back downstairs and out to the patio. "Honey, I—oh, you're not here." She looked around the backyard, then heard something coming from the woods. She leaned forward to listen.

Rustling.

She instinctively backed up. "Probably a deer," she muttered to herself. Then more rustling, a low sounding male voice.

She walked gingerly up to the tree line. Then she heard two voices.

Unmistakably male.

She stopped in her tracks.

Raspy, breathless voices full of desire. She recognized one of them as her son's.

Risa stepped back quickly, her heart thudding. The ground under her feet seemed to undulate.

She heard her son gasp, "Oh God. *Charlie.*"

She staggered her way back to the patio. An invisible hand shoved her down hard onto the chaise lounge, dumbstruck, her mouth open and shaped into a soundless "O".

She was not sure how long she remained outside or when she stood up to go back into the house, but she had somehow made her way to the couch in the darkened living room. Calmly aware of her own breath, slowed now, but still on edge, she replayed the voices she'd heard in the woods.

"No," she whispered. "This can't be."

When the familiar squeak of the back screen door opened, she sat up, her senses in high alert. She debated whether to talk to him now, or just keep it quiet; watch him, assess the situation, perhaps call it a phase, and let it go because surely, he was happy with his girlfriend Deborah, wasn't he? They were the couple to beat at school! They were so *comfortable* with one another! It seemed so perfect. This *had* to be a phase. She understood that teenagers got crushes on members of the same sex that eventually lose steam when they realize it's just another part of growing up. Afterall, she'd had feelings for Betty back in high school. She thought Betty might be fun to make out with, but then Roger came along, and Betty was history.

Unaware of her in the living room, Corey tip-toed around to the steps, climbed them slowly, carrying his sneakers in one hand, grabbing the railing with the other to bear his weight over the known creaks and groans. Risa watched this in fascination. Apparently, he had this late-night routine down pat. She wondered how long this activity had been going on.

She watched him disappear into the darkness of the upper staircase, heard him enter his bedroom and close the door, the latch barely audible.

She quietly expressed a long-held breath.

When she was certain Corey was in for the night, she climbed the steps much as he did, taking care not to make any noise. She entered the master suite, closed the door quietly, and shed her clothes in her dressing room. Her nightly regime of cold crème and facial moisturizer coupled with a pluck here and there of stray eyebrow hairs went unaccomplished. Instead, she climbed into bed settling herself on her side to spoon with her husband. When he felt her, he moaned, adjusted his position, took her arm in his hand, then fell back to sleep.

She lay unmoving, her mind racing.

## CHAPTER TWO

After a restless night's sleep, Risa arose and padded downstairs for her first cup of coffee. Rachel was in the kitchen having breakfast.

"Hi, Mom."

Risa bent down to kiss her daughter's head. "Hi, honey, how did you sleep?"

"Good, you?"

"Eh, not so great."

Rachel stopped eating her cereal long enough to ask, "How come?"

Risa reset the coffee machine with a fresh filter of grounds. "Oh, I don't know. Just getting old I guess."

"Mom! You're not old at all!"

Risa crossed her arms over her chest and leaned against the counter. "You're up earlier than usual! What's your plan today?"

"Nan's mom is taking us to the country club to watch the regatta. It starts at noon but she's picking me up at eleven. I think we're going to have lunch afterwards."

"Sounds like fun. Is Corey up? I see the car is still in the driveway. He was supposed to take it in for a tune up."

"Oh, he's already gone."

Risa stood up straighter. "He is? Where did he go?"

"I don't know. Somewhere with that guy Charlie. Said he'd be back around lunchtime."

"Charlie?" Her breath caught in her chest.

"Yeah, Charlie…whatshisname. Don't you remember him? He was here at Corey's graduation party last week. Kind of quiet. Maybe kind of nerdy. I think he's kind of cute. Actually."

Risa tried to remember. "There were so many people here, I can't place him."

"Red hair, glasses, medium sized, nice smile."

Risa poured her coffee. "Is he a good friend of Corey's?"

"Mom, why the third degree?"

Risa sat down opposite her daughter. The light streaming in through the large bay window in the breakfast nook was warm, but Risa felt a chill. She explained, "I just like to know who you two spend time with. Is that so awful?"

"I guess not. Are you mad at him or something?"

"Why would you think that?"

"I don't know. You seem kind of weird this morning." Rachel pushed her chair back from the table.

Risa smiled thinly. "Don't scrape, please. I'm fine, honey."

"Oops, sorry mom. Okay, I'm going to get ready." She rinsed her bowl in the sink then made for the stairs.

When Rachel was out of earshot, Risa went to the wall phone and dialed Peg's number.

"Berkowitz residence."

"Oh, hi. Edith. Is Mrs. Berkowitz available? It's Mrs. Shapiro."

"Oh, hello Mrs. S. I think she's just now out of the tub. Can I have her call you right back?"

"Please. Thank you."

"Of course. Have a nice day now."

"You, too."

Risa hung up and paced the kitchen, telling herself to get a grip, not entirely sure what motivated her to call Peg. "Panic, desperation?" she said to the empty kitchen. "There's *got* to be an explanation for all of this." She poured herself another cup of coffee.

When the phone rang, she jumped, slopping coffee onto her robe. "Oh, damn it," she muttered while reaching for a paper towel. She grabbed the receiver, "Hello?"

"Hi, you called?"

"Yes."

"Hey, what's going on, you don't sound like yourself?"

"I just spilled coffee all over the place."

"Do you want to call me back?"

"No…" She sat down hard in a chair.

"Is everything alright?" Peg asked in a gentle, concerned voice.

"No. I think..." She stopped short. Instead, she said, "I think I'm just having a bad period, is all."

"Ah! Okay, I have the perfect antidote, *as you know*! Lunch, shopping, and drinks—lots of drinks—after. And who better to do that with than me?" Peg laughed.

Risa nodded, "You *are* my go-to for that and it sounds utterly perfect, but I have ten scripts to read by Friday and the clock is ticking. How about a raincheck?"

Peg said, "Well, okay. But you *really* don't sound like yourself. Are you sure everything is alright?"

Risa fought the urge again. *Don't jump the gun*, she told herself. "I'm good." She switched gears. "Any gossip I should know about?"

"Did you hear about Connie and Stan?"

Glad for the diversion, she answered, "No, what's going on?"

"She caught him red-handed with his pants down, and I'm here to tell you it was *not* in their bedroom!"

"Stanley? Who would want to get near him, he's such a schlub!"

"Apparently, this bimbo who works at the watering hole where he goes with his pals after work."

"Is she going to divorce him?"

"Oh, no. I got the whole story last night at the club. I was waiting for Walt to meet me for dinner, but he had a last-minute emergency, so I went to the bar for a glass of wine. Well, if she didn't march up and park herself next to me! Honestly, she was already three-sheets! She spilled the beans for half an hour. Said she'd never divorce him because she worked too hard for his money. Instead, she went to a shrink!"

"A shrink? What for?"

"Because she was afraid she might kill him in his sleep some night!"

Risa chuckled, "Such drama. So, where did she find this shrink?"

"She wanted someone out of town so no one would recognize her. I think she went three times. Someone in Salem.

Alice something, but then again, she was tanked. Who knows what's real."

Risa was ready to end the conversation. "Okay, well, let's hope she doesn't kill him off yet. I'm going to let you go. Let's do lunch and shopping next week?"

"Okay, it's a date."

When they disconnected, Risa sat still for a moment, then reached for the yellow pages; perhaps the call to Peg was serendipitous.

She looked up therapists in Salem. Out of six listed, only one was a woman.

Alice Stern, Board Certified Licensed Social Worker.

\*\*\*

An hour later, the front door opened. Risa was in the kitchen wiping down an already spotless counter.

"Hey, mom!" Corey ambled to the fridge.

"Where were you?" She threw the paper towel into the trash container.

He shoved his sunglasses up onto the top of his head. "Out with a few friends, how come?" He turned to face her; his hand stopped in mid-air with a can of soda. "Mom?"

Icily, she said, "Please, sit down."

He set the drink back into the fridge, closed the door, and gingerly pulled a chair out from the kitchenette table. "Okay."

Risa squared her shoulders. "Who is Charlie?"

Corey blanched. "Charlie?"

"Yes, who is Charlie?"

He cleared his throat. "Just a friend from school."

Risa was shaking inside. She crossed her arms in front of her chest to steady herself, then said, matter-of-factly, "Who were you in the woods with last night?"

Corey stammered, "What? I was with you! And then you went to bed. And I…oh, God, mom. Did you—"

Risa cut him off. "Yes. I heard you."

"Oh, God." His voice was barely audible. His shoulders slunk and he held his head.

"How long has this been going on?" Her insides continued to shake involuntarily.

"Just the once, last night, I swear."

"Why, Corey? Why?" She paced to ward off raw nerves.

He turned his body away from her, his sunglasses falling to the table. "I don't even know…you wouldn't understand… I can't…" He stifled a cry.

His shoulders shook, he started to whimper. "Mom, I am so ashamed. You should have never…"

Her love for him took charge and she slowly approached him, took his hands from his face, and pulled him into her arms. "Let's talk this out, can we?"

He nodded, his face against her waist as if he were a child. "Does dad know?"

"No, he does not. And let's just leave it that way."

This seemed to mollify him. "Thank you, mom, I am so sorry that you had to…hear that."

She nodded, "I am too. But let's start at the beginning, okay?"

"Okay."

She reached for a tissue from a box on the counter, gave it to him, waited for him to compose himself, then asked, "Where did you meet this young man?"

"In science class. He's the smart type, you know?" He played with his sunglasses on the table, shoving them this way and that.

"You're smart, too."

He sniffled. "Maybe. He offered to tutor me after school because I was worried about the final exam. For some reason, he really took a liking to me. He said I was easy to talk to, that he was having problems at home with his father. I guess his father drinks a lot and slaps him around."

"Oh, that's terrible!"

"He has bruises all up and down his arms. That's why he always wears long-sleeved shirts. I felt so bad for him."

"I'm sure you did. You're a very caring young man."

"Thanks, mom." He wiped his nose. "Maybe too caring. Anyhow, we just started talking, we'd take walks together around the track at school. He walked me home a few times."

"Where does he live?"

"Opposite end of town from us."

Risa understood what that meant. "Long way for him to get home."

"He rides his bicycle everywhere."

She asked, "What made you want to take the friendship elsewhere?"

"I don't know. It just kind of happened."

"Well, I'm not sure how happy I am with that answer." She looked him square in the eye. "Do you think you might be—"

He answered abruptly. "God *no* mom! No *way!* I mean, what happened with Charlie is *over*. I told him this morning that it can't go further! I have a girlfriend and I am happy with her!"

Without warning Risa experienced a jarring, vertiginous shift that moved right down into her soul. She steadied herself on the kitchen counter, averting her eyes from Corey's. The truth was in his eyes. All she could muster was, "Well, I don't have to tell you I am happy to hear *that*."

Corey's look was pleading. "And we won't tell dad?"

Risa struggled with the concept of betraying her husband about something like this, but she needed time to sort it all out.

She regarded her son with a troubled set of eyes. Her maternal curiosity about his intimate life with someone of the opposite sex seemed natural. But this new twist went beyond natural curiosity, it was out of her scope of what she deemed normal. She relented. "Our secret, for now."

He reached for her hand and gripped it, color returning to his face. "I love you."

# CHAPTER THREE

All the following week, Risa watched Corey closely. He brought Deborah to the house every day, focusing on her every need. There were no more trips to the woods or 'meetings' elsewhere that she knew of. And while Corey appeared normal to Saul and Rachel, Risa felt he was overcompensating.

She knew bad acting when she saw it.

She wavered with the idea of calling Alice. What would she say to her? She never had the need or thought to seek out a therapist. Everything in her life, including the day to day 'disasters' with growing children, ran smoothly. Her blessings were many. She was fortunate to marry a man who was her soulmate and took such good care of her and their children. Her theatre arts degree from Radcliffe College afforded her a place in one of the more well-funded community theatres, the Cape Ann Playhouse. After a year of solid box-office hits, she no longer needed to audition for roles, gaining company status. She was asked to sit on the Board of CAP as the assistant Creative Director, a role which she took very seriously.

But what she did *not* have was a barometer for something that could upset the balance of home. And there was no one Risa felt comfortable enough to talk with about it except for someone who did not know her or her family.

Alice Stern.

She finally placed the call on a Monday and was given an appointment on that Thursday. Between those days, she hemmed and hawed about canceling the meeting. But the nagging truth lay bare the day she confronted Corey about his transgression.

It was not going to go away whether she willed it to or not.

And she could act only so long.

# Letters to Corey

# CHAPTER FOUR

*July 1980*

Risa took the most direct route to Salem, found Alice Stern's office, which appeared to be in a house, and checked the address again to make sure it was correct. The sign at the apron of the driveway directed clients to the back of the house, where there was parking and a back entrance.

She approached the door and followed the instructions near the buzzer. A moment later, a woman opened the door. Her smile was warm as she said, "You must be Mrs. Shapiro?"

Risa responded, "Yes, I am. And you are Alice Stern?"

"I am! Please, come on in."

Risa followed her down a short hallway into an office. It was small and nicely appointed, homey yet professional.

Alice extended her arm toward a worn, soft leather couch. "Please, have a seat! By the way, has anyone ever told you that you look like Anne Bancroft?"

Risa chuckled, "Many times. It's a toss-up, though, as to who has the bigger nose!" She sat down on the edge of the couch, her purse in her lap.

Alice sat down in a wingback chair across from Risa, adjusted glasses that sat midway between the tip and top of her nose, reached for her pad and pen then asked, "So, what brings you here today?"

Risa opened her mouth to speak, but nothing came out. She pursed her lips then cleared her throat. "Well, you see, I'm new at this and I have no idea what to do or expect."

Alice nodded. "It's not unusual to feel that way. How about we lay the groundwork for what you can expect from me. Would that work, Mrs. Shapiro?"

"Yes, and please call me Risa."

"Okay, Risa. I am a board-certified social worker with a master's degree from Harvard University. I've been in business now for over twelve years. The hour you are here is entirely yours, meaning you have free reign to do or say what you need. I will listen, take notes, ask you questions, and make suggestions. What I will *not* do is talk about myself or become distracted. Your information is private according to the law, and if at any time you would like to stop our sessions, your file will be stored in an archival vault in my basement. Does this sound good, so far?"

Risa shifted her position. She realized she had been sitting stock-still, barely breathing. She nodded. "I think that sounds good, Alice."

"Okay! We've cleared the first roadblock!"

"So, where do we go from here?"

"Let's start by finding out what brought you here today."

"Okay. I needed someone to talk to."

Alice waited.

"Something happened recently that I..."

Alice nodded for her to continue.

"Things are changing in my life. Without my permission."

Alice started taking notes. "What kinds of things are changing?"

"I thought I would never have to do this; talk to someone I did not know."

"That is the beauty of therapy, Risa. It is completely objective and subjective at the same time. What we discuss must be about you. Sure, other people will come and go from the conversations, and we might even spend an entire session about that one person, but what really counts in here, Risa, is how *you* feel."

"Okay, that seems fair enough." She was starting to relax. "Do you work with certain types of..."

With her pen poised just above the pad, Alice asked, "Certain types of?"

Risa blurted, "I think my son is a homosexual."

Alice nodded, jotted down a few notes, then sat back in her chair. "Okay. That was brave. Would you like to start at the beginning?"

Risa swallowed, hard. She withdrew a tissue from one of the three Kleenex boxes placed strategically around the sitting area. "Well, I caught him with another boy in the woods behind our house last week."

"What were they doing?"

"I didn't see them; I could only hear them. And it was clearly…lustful."

"And how did that make you feel?" Alice's voice was quiet, soothing.

"Like I was in a dream. Shocked." She crumpled the tissue in her palm.

"Can you tell me a little about your son."

"His name is Corey, he'll be eighteen in October, he's going to go to New York University in the fall."

"Has he shown interest in girls?"

"Oh yes, he has a steady, her name is Deborah."

"Does he seem happy with her?"

"He does! They are always together."

"So, after the incident of last week, did you speak with him about it?"

"I did. The day after it happened."

"Did you speak with your husband about it?"

"No."

"Why is that?"

"He's not fond of homosexuality."

"I see. Is there anyone else you feel comfortable talking to about this?"

"I almost told my best friend, but then I didn't."

"Oh? What stopped you?"

"I don't know. It just didn't feel right, I guess. I didn't want to—" Suddenly, she stood up. "You know, to tell you the truth maybe I made a hasty decision to come here. Corey assured me that the experience was a one-time thing. And I need to believe him."

Alice looked up. "Why do you have to believe him?"

Risa felt defensive. "He is my *son*. If he says it's a one-time thing, I believe him!" She did not disclose that she saw a deeper truth in his eyes that day.

"But…do you?" Alice reached for a glass of water from her side table and took a sip.

"Of course, I do! Look, you're a lovely woman, and indeed well educated, but I think I can handle this on my own."

Alice shrugged. "It's your hour, Risa."

"Well, I'll go ahead and pay for the hour. I don't want to waste your time. What do I owe you?" She reached into her purse for her wallet, withdrew it, then stopped midway.

Alice set her pen and paper on the small end table next to her chair. "Would you say you made this appointment after some thought, since the incident occurred last week?"

"Yes."

"You drove here from where?"

"Manchester."

"Okay, not right around the corner. So, you had some time during the drive to reconsider, yet here we are."

The women stared at each other for a moment. Risa sighed heavily, dropped her wallet back into her purse, then sat back down on the couch. "Yes, here we are." After a moment, she stated, "What I need is information. I know nothing about homosexuality. I should have gone into Boston to the public library there."

"Information is surely a great tool, and to your advantage." Alice said then added, "But let's keep going here for the hour, okay?"

Risa relented. "Okay."

Alice picked up her pad and pen again. "Let's talk a little about your relationship with Corey."

Risa chuckled. "We're going to need more than an hour for *that* explanation!

"I can certainly appreciate that! Do you have any other children, Risa?"

"I have a daughter named Rachel. She is four years younger than Corey."

"Did you experience any post-partum depression after either child?"

"Yes, with Corey. Not so much with Rachel. I knew what to expect."

"How long did it last?"

She thought for a moment then said, "Well, it was four

months after he was born. Late February. I will never forget this, Alice. It was in the middle of the night, and I thought I heard Corey crying so I quickly went into the nursery. But he was just moving around in his crib, not crying." She looked out the window over Alice's desk, reliving the memory. "I picked him up and took him in my arms to the rocking chair. I looked down at him and something came over me. It was like a warm, strong hand reaching right into my heart! In the dim light, I *saw* him differently, almost like I was seeing him for the first time. I felt a love so deep and profound, that all I could do was cry. A tear dropped onto his cheek, and I wiped it away before it could slip down into his ear. I told him—this beautiful little bundle in my arms—that he and I would do great things together. That I would give him the world, love him unconditionally, no matter what."

Alice had been taking notes. She looked up from her pad. "How positively beautiful." She smiled then asked, "And?"

"And ever since that night, I came back to myself."

"The firstborn is typically the special one. Would you say that you and Corey are close?"

"Very."

"And Saul, is he as close to Corey as you are?"

"No." Then added quickly, "But that's not to say he doesn't love him."

"Of course. What does your husband do?"

"He is an attorney."

"Was he home during Corey's younger years?"

"As much as he could be. He was made junior partner at his father's law firm in Boston right after I got pregnant. You see, we tried to wait to start the family, what with his workload. Best laid plans, right? But yes he was very attentive and present during my pregnancy."

"Would you say your husband has a good influence on Corey?"

Risa thought about this for a moment. "He does."

"I noticed a hesitation. Are you sure of your answer?"

"Yes." Was all she wanted to say.

"Who were some of the other influences in Corey's life?"

Risa smiled, "My parents."

"Tell me a little about them?"

"My father, Abe. He is the first violist in the Boston Symphony Orchestra and a professor of theory at the New England Conservatory of Music. He is as gentle and loving as they come. My mother, Ruthie, mainly raised us three girls—I have two younger sisters—and did seamstress work on the side. It was a wonderful family to grow up in and Corey adores them. They doted on him when he was a baby and youngster, now they treat him like a mature young man. He so enjoys spending time with them."

"And what about Saul's parents?"

Risa snorted. "Hmph. That's a whole different story."

"In a nutshell."

"They are ridiculously wealthy, live in a mansion just a mile from us, are not warm and fuzzy by any stretch, and basically 'bought' his childhood. He tolerates them now out of respect for his dad. But Nathan and Elaine Shapiro are cut from an entirely different cloth than us. It was and still is hard to believe Saul came from that family. He's nothing like them. He fits in very well with my family and has from the get-go."

"So, to recap, Corey's main influence is you, then?"

"I would say so. I've exposed him to many things. Some of those things were a hard sell to Saul but, we managed to placate him."

"Placate? What do you mean by hard sell?"

"Well, without going into too much detail, suffice it to say that some of the things I exposed Corey to were less than…manly."

Alice nodded, "Can you elaborate?"

Risa took a deep breath then let it out through her nose. "Not today. I think I just need to get up to speed and try to understand this situation."

Alice looked at her watch. "Our time is almost up. I want to give you a few books about homosexuality. You might find the language a bit technical, but you'll get the drift." She stood and headed toward the bookcase. "You realize that homosexuality is not a choice. It's in our DNA. Many parents expose their children to a wide variety of so-called male-female experiences in life. It makes for a well-rounded child. Some parents feel that boys should be boys and girls should be girls." She pulled a book from the case then asked, "Would you like to make another appointment?"

Risa stammered, "So, you *do* think I need to come back?"

Alice turned to face her and smiled. "Yes, you have to return my books."

Risa relented. "You're a straight shooter, aren't you?"

Alice ran her fingers along the spines of the books until she reached the title she was looking for. "I am. And, truth be known, I have a good sense about you, Mrs. Shapiro. I get the feeling you are a straight shooter as well."

Risa took cash out of her wallet. "I'd like to think I am. I don't like to mince words. How much for today?"

"An hour session is sixty."

She counted out the cash then said, "Okay. Should I make the appointment with your secretary?"

"I don't have a secretary. The number you called is a service. They only make or cancel appointments. But I have my schedule right here and I will call them to fill the block." She found the other book she was looking for. "Here you go. These will give you a good start." She handed Risa the books then walked to her desk and picked up her appointment book. "Same day and time for next week?"

"As far as I know. Yes, let's do that."

"Let me give you a card."

"No, I'll remember." She didn't want any evidence of her visit to Alice to get into the wrong hands. As it was, she would have to find a place to hide the books.

On the way out of the office, Alice said, "And by the way, Anne Bancroft's nose is bigger."

Risa laughed, feeling better about having come to Alice; having stayed through the hour and setting up another appointment.

She felt she had an ally.

One that nobody would ever have to know about.

For now.

THERAPY NOTE:
*Risa Shapiro: Well-dressed woman of means, poised, articulate, 2 children, husband, reluctant to be here at first, believes her son is homosexual. Mother/son relationship very significant. Reading material re: homosexuality supplied. Another appt made for the following week. AS*

## CHAPTER FIVE

Risa found herself parked at the harbor in Marblehead instead of going directly home. Her thoughts were too scattered.

She faced the inlet, watching the activity. The air was thick with a heady summer brine, and the rhythmic clank of mast sails shifting in the light breeze gave her a moment to steady her nerves.

She picked up one of the books Alice had loaned her, then murmured, "I can do this. Just a simple lane change is all."

She scanned the table of contents. "Oy vey." Then started with the Preface.

*While homosexuality is considered an aberrant behavior, the findings of the APA do not parallel societal views regarding the proclivities of males and females who cannot physically or emotionally love someone of the opposite sex. Since homosexuality is gene related, there can be—*

Risa looked up from the book. "Who in *my* family? In Saul's?" She continued.

*If you are a parent of a homosexual child, it is not only frightening, but confusing at best. In this book, we will attempt to dispel the myth that homosexuality is a chosen desire. And while we, as parents, want the best for our children, we must understand the basic building blocks that differentiate one child from another. It starts early...parents might blame themselves...guilt hides the truth...shame is apparent...*

And on it went.

Risa closed the book and looked out the window. "I can't do this."

The tranquility of the harbor did not assuage her building anxiety. Their lives were going along at a comfortable pace, everyone doing what they needed to do, everyone seemingly happy.

This was not just a simple lane change; it was a detour into an unknown.

# Letters to Corey

# CHAPTER SIX

*The office of Alice Stern*
*The following week*

Risa sat down on the couch setting the loaned books on the table in front of her.

Alice asked, "How are you today, Risa?"

"I don't really know. I had my thoughts organized until I pulled into your driveway."

"How about we start with how your week was since our last session?"

"It was okay, I suppose." She hesitated, cleared her throat, then asked. "I have a question."

"Okay."

"Are we just going to focus on the matter of Corey's sexuality?"

Alice nodded and said, "A good question. I think the important thing to keep in mind is that we are here for you. Your son's sexuality is the impetus for your visits, but you are here to discover and deal with your own feelings around this issue."

"So, we *are* going to…analyze me?"

Alice nodded slightly and smiled, "In a fashion, yes. If we are going to make headway with Corey, we may have to."

"But I'm not sure I want to go into all of that."

Alice picked up her pen and pad. "What did you think of the books? Were you able to glean any information to help you understand?"

"Not really. Maybe some. I'm looking for ways to *deal* with this problem."

"Isn't that why you're here?"

"I feel like this is going to take a long time in here. I need something I can grasp onto *now*. The day to day."

Alice asked, "Have you had more conversations with Corey regarding what happened?"

"No, I have not. He seems to be behaving himself. But I can

see through his façade."

"So, you're conflicted?"

Risa sighed heavily. "Oh, God, I don't know." She shook her head and focused on the bookcase.

Alice asked gently, "What do you fear most, Risa?"

"That..." she reached for a tissue, snapping it out of the box and bringing it to her eyes. "Damn it all."

Alice waited for Risa to compose herself then said, "How about we break a few things down?"

"Please. I need to make sense of this and soon."

Alice leaned forward a bit. "Paint me a picture of your life at home."

"Oh, it's pretty normal, like any family; we have our ups and downs, our routines."

"So, if Corey is truly homosexual, what reactions could you expect from your family?"

Risa harumphed and shook her head slightly. "I cannot even imagine what it would do. It would not go well. I think my husband would be devastated. He has his business and reputation to think of." She hesitated then added, "The Shapiro families are very prominent not only in Manchester but, right down to Boston. It would cause a significant scandal."

"Okay, so what scares you more? Your husband finding out about it, or the reputation of your family?"

"Both."

"Why do you think your husband would be devastated?"

"Because he is not fond of male homosexuality. He finds it repulsive."

"Those are strong descriptors, Risa. Do you think he may have had an experience of his own?"

Risa sat up and said emphatically, "Absolutely not!"

"I get that you are angry. Who are you angry at?"

"I'm not angry. I'm just..." she dabbed at her eyes again.

Alice shuffled her papers. "You mentioned something in our last session that I would like to address. You said you and Corey did many things together during his formative years. Do you feel, in some way, that the things you did together might have influenced him in certain ways?"

Risa looked down into her lap, fussing with the tissue. She said in a quiet voice, "Oh, I imagine there were many. Saul used to get mad at me for exposing him to…well…to…"

Alice waited.

She looked up and stated, "I used to take him clothes shopping with me. He was eight or nine years old. I'd bring him into the dressing room with me and he would tell me what worked and what didn't. He had a very discerning eye. He loved the feel of the fabric. He had a good sense of color." Risa hesitated then sat forward and asked, "Do you think my exposing him to things less manly made him homosexual? The books said it's already built into his DNA."

Alice nodded. "The books are correct. I'm just trying to get a picture of why Saul would be upset about you exposing him to things less manly. Were there other things?"

Risa nodded. "He was very active in my theatre work. He was serious and focused with helping me learn my lines at home, went to the theatre with me for rehearsals—showed interest in the backstage goings-on. He liked to think he was my leading man. He'd read the lines with such concentration!"

"Were there any actors Corey took a liking to?"

Risa nodded. "There were several, but he seemed to focus a lot of attention on a talented, spirited young man named Devin."

"Was Devin homosexual?"

"Yes."

"And did Saul have any opinions about Devin, did he condone Corey spending time around him?"

"Saul often chided me about Corey taking so much of an interest in the theatre. He wanted Corey to get into sports, camping, or to go fishing."

"Did Saul encourage these things with Corey?"

"They went on a camping trip with my father and Uncle Fritzy. Once. He said it was a lot of fun, but probably not something that was for him."

Alice repositioned her glasses on her nose. "So, what else did you two do?"

"Well, we often went into Boston to see matinees. His favorites were musicals. He loved taking the train to town. He had so much fun at Faneuil Hall and the waterfront. It was a pleasure to be with him. He was very curious about things from a young age."

"Would you say he shows an interest in film or acting?"

"Yes, and no. I think he just appreciates it. Saul wants him to study law—which he will never do—or go into business, which, who knows."

"How does all this make you feel?"

"I don't understand. What do you mean, how does all this make me feel?"

"It seems as though you and Saul have differences of opinions regarding Corey. Does this make you feel defensive toward Saul?"

"Sometimes. I feel as though I must defend Corey because I know him so much better than Saul does."

"You spent most of Corey's formative years with him. So, in the current situation, would you say sharing this information with Saul might put too much pressure on Corey right now?"

"I promised him I would not tell his father. But, if it is indeed to be his lifestyle, it is up to him to talk to his father about it. I can protect him for only so long. But I don't like being part of a lie. I've never betrayed my husband before."

"You mentioned you spent the week in turmoil."

"We don't have secrets."

Alice nodded. "Until now."

Risa sighed, leaned her head on the back of the couch, and looked at the ceiling. "That's right, up until now." She brought her gaze back to Alice and asked, "Am I failing Corey? Should I just bring this right out into the open?"

Alice set her pad down on the side table. "It's a tough choice, Risa. You're juggling a lot right now: on one hand, you don't want to upset the sense of normalcy in your home or jostle your social status. And on the other hand, this is something very important to share with your husband and you are afraid to do so because of how he feels about homosexuality. The only thing I can say is this. A child grows up with values given by its parents. Parents, by and large, want to give their children the best education they can—be respectful, give and take, be honest. The textbooks go into minute detail of how our personalities develop but for the sake of our conversation here, let's imagine this from Corey's position: he learns something about himself—and we don't know exactly when this occurred—that already comes with shame and fear of being something less than what we all call normal, and the very real possibilities of disappointment from the rest of his family, from society. Loving someone of the same sex is not a norm, and who knows if it ever will be, but that does not stop it from happening. Perhaps Corey knew about this years ago, maybe started investigating these new feelings behind everyone's back because he knew it was considered wrong. He knows his father will be more than angry, but he knows *you* will be there, unconditionally. So, when you say you think you're failing him, how so?"

"I should have seen the signs! But I didn't! And all this time it was right in front of me!"

Alice responded, "You weren't looking for them. How could you have known?"

Risa shook her head and grabbed another tissue. "This is all so very upsetting. I can't even believe I'm going through this!" She closed her eyes as a sob escaped from her throat. She said quietly, "I don't know how to get through the rest of the summer with this knowledge."

Alice said gently, "This is why you are here. To make sense of your next steps. Unfortunately, I cannot change what's happening, but again, we can keep you focused and informed."

Risa nodded while blowing her nose. "I know."

"Are you able to keep your emotions in check at home?"

Risa chuckled mirthlessly, "I'm an actress, I know how to do that. I don't think anyone is wiser. Well, that's not entirely true. Saul asked me the other night if anything was bothering me and I told him I was nervous and sad that Corey was heading off to school in the fall. Our first empty nester and all…"

"I'm sure that is part of it." Alice asked, "Would it be prudent for you to take Corey aside before he leaves for college and lay it on the line?"

"And say what? Ask him if he is a homosexual? He would deny it, like he did a few weeks ago. I'm not sure what that would do." She shook her head. "No, I feel like I am at a standstill. It's a teeter-totter. I don't know."

"Let's keep going along as we've been, at least you can come here and sort it all out."

"I agree."

"Same time next week?"

"Yes."

*THERAPY NOTE:*

*Making headway. She has kept this information from her husband—homosexuality could be familial/reputation breaking point. Will continue to peel back the layers. Also, her husband is repulsed by male homosexuality. Risa strongly denies that he has had an experience and is sure he would have told her about it. Interesting comparison as Risa is reluctant to talk to Saul about Corey. AS*

## CHAPTER SEVEN

*Rubin Hall*
*New York City*
*August 1980*

"Of course, he's on the tenth floor!" Saul muttered to himself and grunted as he hauled the last of the packed boxes through the crowded lobby. More than six hundred freshmen were in transition. The parking lot of the dorm overflowed to the street; people bustled, fathers calling out orders to family members, wives taking one thing at a time to the elevators which were slow and threatening to stop all together. Luckily, the weather co-operated, the rain held off. But it was sticky, humid and without a breeze.

Risa held onto her son in the parking lot. She whispered into his neck, "I don't even know what to say, Corey. I'm so proud of you, yet I feel like you're still too young to be on your own."

"Mom, I'm going to be fine. You'll see. I always get around, right?"

"You do," she managed to say through a tight throat. She leaned back and habitually moved his long bangs away from his eyes then cupped his face in her hand. "Such a beautiful boy. Please be careful." She said this quietly, her heart aching.

Corey took her hand in his and pressed it to his face. He whispered back, "I will mom. I love you."

She already felt him disconnect. She watched his eyes dance with possibilities. She had to let go of him. She choked back a sob and quickly reached for a hanky from her skirt pocket. "I…"

Saul came out of the building, took his son into a bear hug. "Okay, you're in! This is it, Core, you're ready for the next chapter in your life. I'm very proud of you, son. The house won't be the same without you. I'll miss you." He reached for his wallet, "Now do you have enough cash?"

"I'm good, dad, thank you."

"Okay. Well, did I already tell you I am going to miss

you?"

"You did. Me too."

A group of students approached Saul, Risa, and Corey. Risa had been watching them on and off as they handed out pamphlets to groups of people in the parking lot.

A tall, nice-looking boy smiled and said to Corey, "Hey there! Are you an incoming freshman?"

"Yes, I am!"

The boy held out his hand. "I'm Teddy from the GLF. We're having a rally tomorrow night outside the Parker House. The directions are on the handout."

Corey smiled and shook his hand, "I'm Corey Shapiro. What's the GLF?"

Ted took on a serious voice. "It's the Gay Liberation Front. Never forget Stonewall."

Corey's smile dropped.

Risa's smile dropped.

Saul stepped forward. "The Gay Liberation Front? What do you mean by that?"

Ted said, "The Gay Liberation Front, man. Don't you know about us?"

"No, I'm afraid we don't. My son probably isn't interested in this."

Ted looked from Saul to Corey, then to Risa—who was glad she had sunglasses on. She was horrified. She watched as the other two boys eyed Corey up and down.

Ted challenged Saul. "Well, maybe your son might be interested in our cause."

Saul gave the pamphlet back to Ted. "I think not."

Ted took it then handed it back to Corey and said directly. "If you ever want to know what the GLF is about, we're always in need of people. Straight or gay, okay? We rally in peace!"

Corey nodded and took the handout. When Ted and his pals went on to the next group, Saul said under his breath, "Of all the nerve."

Risa redirected Corey and Saul away from the threesome. She tried to sound upbeat. "Go on, you. Time for *us* to head back north and *you* to your new life!"

After an awkward silence and hug, Corey nodded quickly and said, "It's that time, isn't it! Well, okay! You guys drive safely back north."

Corey turned to go as Risa blew him a kiss.

Saul held her around the shoulders as he guided her back to the car. "Navigate for me?"

She mumbled, "Of course." She blew her nose, took one more look at the high-rise where her son would live for the first year of his college career and watched him disappear into the melee.

Once out of the parking lot, she focused her attentions on the map of the city. As soon as they fought their way back to I-75, Risa stowed the map in the glovebox, sat back, and closed her eyes. She was so tired.

Saul reached for her hand and said gently, "Well, it's just you, me, and Rachel now in that big old house now. It's going to be different, don't you think?" He shifted lanes and swore under his breath at someone who cut in front of him.

Quietly she responded, "Yes, it will be."

"You're going to be fine, honey." Saul's voice was soothing.

She replayed the scene in the parking lot, her throat constricting once again.

"Honey?" He stole a glance at her.

"I'm okay. Just…" she pulled a fresh tissue from a box on the floor. Her tears were hot on her cheeks. Saul gripped her hand a little tighter. For a moment, she thought she might just blurt it out, share her suspicions. But she focused on the road ahead, on the cars weaving in and out of traffic on the highway.

After a while in companionable silence, Saul asked, "Would you like to stop in Mystic for dinner?"

"How long do we have?"

"At least two and a half hours. Why don't you take a nap?"

"I think I will."

"Will the radio bother you? Detroit is playing Boston."

"No honey, it won't bother me." She put her head back and closed her swollen eyes, the chatter of over-zealous sportscasters preferable to the noise in her head. She eventually drifted off.

By the time she stirred, Saul was pulling into the parking lot of Mystic Seafood. She sat up abruptly, "Did I just sleep two hours?"

"You did, sweetheart. Hey, I've got to jump out. My bladder is ready to burst. I'll meet you inside, get us a table?"

"Of course."

Risa pulled the sun visor down taking inventory of her face and hair. She fluffed, reapplied lipstick, rubbed the sleep from her cheeks, and went into the restaurant. She felt oddly unbalanced.

When Saul found her at their table, she regarded him. "Maybe we should get a hotel room, you look dog tired honey. How many miles are we from Manchester?"

"Oh, I'd say another three hours. There was a Holiday Inn right off the freeway. Maybe we should call it a day, start fresh in the morning. Will Ellie's parents mind if Rachel spends the night?"

"I'm sure Lois will be fine. I'll call her now. I want to touch base with Rachel anyhow, she'll want to know how it went with Corey. Why don't you order me the fresh catch of the day?"

"You want some wine?"

"If we aren't going to drive, let's split a bottle, maybe even two. We've earned it."

He smiled, "There's my girl."

They leisured over dinner, Risa finally relaxed. Their conversation was fun, light, reminiscent of the old days before they had kids. She put the stress of the summer behind her. It was Corey's game now. She would no longer have to run defense. No longer need to lie to Saul.

Out of sight, out of mind.

By the time they left the restaurant and checked into the hotel, they quickly showered and slipped between the clean, taut sheets. Risa snuggled in close with Saul, feeling the safety of his love. Before she fell asleep, a thought drifted into her mind. She never believed, in her lifetime, she would need to seek the help of a therapist.

But then again, she never believed in her lifetime that her son would turn out to be anything but normal, either.

# CHAPTER EIGHT

*The Office of Alice Stern*

Risa settled back onto the couch. She joked, "This is getting quite familiar!"

Alice smiled then assumed her position in the high-backed chair. "How are you today, Risa?"

"I'm betwixt and between. We dropped Corey off at school on Saturday. It was crazy. Imagine six hundred students converging…oy, what a mess!"

"I sure can! How did it go?"

"It was fine until a couple of boys approached us, inviting Corey to come to a rally for something called the GLF."

"Oh, yes, the Gay Liberation Front."

Risa's eyes widened. "Do you know about this?"

Alice shrugged, "It's not taboo, you know. The GLF has been in the news since nineteen seventy one."

Risa asked, "Well, where in the hell have *I* been?"

Instead of answering her, Alice asked, "Was Saul with you when this happened?"

"He was! And he firmly told the boys Corey would not be interested in this."

"And you? Did you say anything?"

"I did not. I didn't trust myself."

"As in?"

"As in I did not trust myself. I mean, Alice, really! What was I supposed to say? It happened so quickly, so unexpectedly!"

"Did Corey seem interested?"

"I think he was just as speechless as I was. But I did notice something he did when he thought we'd already gotten in the car to leave."

"What was that?"

"He made to throw the pamphlet away in the trash container but thought about it for a moment then shoved it into his back pocket before he went into the building. Saul had already started the car."

"How does all this make you feel?

"I'm terrified for him."

"How so?"

"He is in one of the biggest cities in the country. While the opportunities are bottomless, so is the population. Do you know what I mean?"

"Yes, New York City is a melting pot for the sexual revolution."

Risa looked off. "I felt like I was leaving him at the mouth of the lion."

"Interesting metaphor."

"Like you said, I can't protect him. Or change him."

"And you've still not said anything to Saul?"

"No, I have not."

"How does that feel?"

"I must admit that things are a bit easier now that he's out of the house."

Alice jotted a few notes then said, "Let's talk about secrets for a moment. Look at them as reference points. One of the frailties of the human condition is that we all keep secrets; maybe to hide something that could make us look bad, weak. Or perhaps to save someone we love or care about from an ugly admission. But who are we saving? Do secrets have the elements of betrayal and omission, shame? It is quite subjective, Risa. A person might keep a secret because he or she feels no one else needs to know about it, as you are experiencing right now, a surface secret which could strike deep at any moment. You want to protect your son. It is most understandable, but at what cost?"

"You think I should tell Saul, *regardless* of the fall-out, right?"

"The choice is yours, Risa. Like I said, I am here to listen, not to judge, but also to dig a little deeper."

Risa cleared her throat, feeling a pang of guilt. She swallowed it down quickly and said, "I'm not sure I want to upset the apple cart just now. I just want, need, normalcy."

Alice simply nodded.

*THERAPY NOTE:*
*Stage one denial.*
*AS*

Letters to Corey

## CHAPTER NINE

*Manchester, MA*
*Fall 1980*

Summer slid into Fall as only it can in New England. After a brief hot spell, the temps slowly dropped into the sixties during the day and fifties at night. Since there was a lot of rain during July and August, the leaf color was magnificent by early October.

The Cape Ann Playhouse season was up and running with Neil Simon's *The Prisoner of Second Avenue*, with Risa in the lead role of Edna Edison. The run was from November 1st through Dec 1st. Risa had reserved an entire section of the house for her family, extended family, and close friends for the Friday night show, then everyone would meet back in Manchester for a cast party afterwards.

As was customary after a performance, the cast appeared in a small room off to the side of the main stage and lobby to receive guests. When Risa stepped out of the stage door, she was barraged with applause, hugs, kisses, and small talk. While she was indulged with audience members singing her praises, she felt a hand on her shoulder and a voice say, "Miss Bancroft?"

She turned, saw who it was, and smiled big. "Devin Lacey! Oh my God, Dev!"

He pulled her into a big hug. "You were *absolutely* marvelous, Reese. What a show!"

Risa stepped back at arm's length. "What are you doing here? I mean, not *here* but in town. I thought you were in New York?"

"I'm in Boston for rehearsals. *Glengarry Glen Ross* at the Orpheum. When I saw you were doing *Prisoner*, I had to come."

"Let me look at you!" She saw that he was still as handsome as he was years ago, maybe a little thinner in the face, eyes sunk in a bit more.

Risa saw Corey out of the corner of her eye and signaled for him to come over to her. She took Corey's hand. "Do you remember Devin Lacey? He's in Boston rehearsing a show!"

Corey took Devin's outstretched hand. "I sure do! Hi Devin!"

Devin looked Corey up and down. "Well look at you! All grown up now. In college?"

"I'm at NYU. Where are you? Mom said you were living in California."

"I was. Eh, wasn't for me. Missed the stage. Moved to New York a few years ago, and now I'm touring with an off-Broadway cast at the Orpheum." He continued to eye Corey.

"You're in New York?" Corey smiled big. "Let's get together!"

Risa felt something pass between Devin and her son, a palpable spark of chemistry. They were still holding each other's hand.

It jarred her down to her toes. Everything she had neatly stowed away from the summer found its way to the forefront of her mind again. A dull thud in her chest clouded the height of the show and the audience response. She cleared her throat. "Corey honey, why don't you gather the troops. We need to coordinate the cars back to the house."

Corey slowly withdrew his hand from Devin's, giving it an extra squeeze before stepping away. Not looking at his mother, he said, "Sure mom. It was nice to see you again, Devin."

"Yes, good to see you too, Corey." Devin watched him walk away then turned his eyes back to Risa. He was about to say something when Risa took him about the shoulders and said in a voice loud enough for people standing nearby to hear. "It was *so good* to see you, Dev! Thanks for coming to the show. I'll make sure to get into town to see *Glen Ross*." Then she moved closer to his ear and whispered in a voice she was certain only he would hear loud and clear. "Not. My. Son."

## CHAPTER TEN

Saul helped Risa with her overcoat while the rest of the family assembled outside in the parking lot. He asked her, "Was that Devin I saw you talking with?"

"It was."

"Please tell me you didn't invite him to the party."

"I did not." She would not let what just transpired ruin her evening.

"Thank you."

They walked out into the brisk November air and joined the ranks of cars lined up to drive the twenty-five minutes north to Manchester.

Saul went around to the drivers' side of the car, Risa put her hand on the passenger door handle. She asked Rachel, "Have you seen your brother?"

"He said he left his gloves in the coatroom; he'll be right out."

Devin Lacey was still talking to another one of the actors when Corey approached him. He asked quietly, quickly, "Where are you staying in Boston? I'd like to meet you for lunch."

Devin smiled then shook his head. "Oh, Corey. Not a good idea."

"Why not?"

He said quietly, "Look, your mother is a good woman. I don't know what your story is, but it would be best if we didn't get together."

"I don't understand!"

Devin shrugged his shoulders. "Corey—"

Corey cut him off. "Let me be the judge of that."

Devin hesitated.

Corey ran his fingers along the lapel of Devin's coat. "Nice overcoat. You wear it well."

Devin took Corey's hand down and murmured, "Just call me tomorrow. I'm at the Park Plaza Hotel."

Corey nodded approvingly, winked, and then tapped Devin's chest lightly. "Count on it."

\*\*\*

Risa and Saul slept in. The party had gone on late. By the time the staff left, it was close to three o'clock in the morning. When Risa and Saul made their way downstairs later, Rachel and Corey were busy in the kitchen.

"What smells so good?" they asked in unison.

There were two cups of steaming coffee on the kitchenette. Risa raised her eyebrows. "Well, *well*! To what do we owe this service?"

Corey pulled two chairs out for his parents, a towel over his forearm. "Ah, Madame and Sir Burr, you are just in time for the house specialty!"

Rachel rolled her eyes. "Oh, brother."

Saul said, "You still think I look like Raymond Burr? He's kind of heavy, isn't he? What's he up to nowadays anyhow?"

Corey said, "We get three channels on our community room television. Lots of *Ironsides* re-runs!" He added, "And it's just from the neck up, dad. You've managed to maintain your swimsuit figure."

Risa stroked Saul's morning stubble, "Mmm. So handsome."

Rachel opened the oven. "Uh, Core. I think the frittata is burning."

Risa looked over, "You made a frittata? Where did you learn to make *that*?"

Corey bent down at the stove. "Ah! It's just right!" He grabbed a kitchen mitt, pulled the heavy cast-iron pan from the oven, and said, "*Voila!*"

Risa exclaimed, "Three months in college and he's making frittatas! I didn't know you had cooking appliances in the dorm."

"We don't. A new friend of mine taught me." He sliced two large pie-shaped pieces from the pan, arranged each one on a plate with left-over fruit and croissants from the party, then set them down in front of his parents.

Saul dug in. "This looks terrific!"

Risa asked, "Are you two going to join us?"

Rachel was at the sink, rinsing dishes. "Already ate. I hate to admit it, but it was good. Like, *really* good!"

"I ate too," Corey said. "You two just enjoy. I have to make a quick phone call. Deborah and I are going to get together this afternoon. She went back yesterday, that's why she wasn't at the show last night. She wants to show me her dorm room and the campus."

Saul asked around a mouthful of food, "How is she doing?"

"Good! Settling in. We're just going to hang out with some of her new friends, bum around town, that kind of thing."

Risa sensed Corey was overcompensating again. She tried to sound casual. "Oh? Do you want me to run you into town? We can have some private time?"

Corey's smile faltered for a moment then he recovered, "Oh thanks mom, but I can take the train in. I know you have another show tonight. Crazy Saturday traffic and all. Wouldn't want anything to happen, you know?"

Risa nodded. "Sure, of course."

Corey looked at his father, "There's a one o'clock to the city dad, could you get me to the station?"

"You bet." He wiped his mouth. "That was delicious, thank you son."

Risa felt a needle jab in her craw; something was not quite kosher.

Corey hugged his mother around the shoulders from behind. "You were amazing last night mom. It's so *good* to see you take command of the boards again!"

She took hold of his arms and leaned her head back, momentarily pacified by his show of affection. "Thank you, son. It was so nice to have you in the audience. Just like old times."

He closed his eyes. "Just like old times."

Letters to Corey

# CHAPTER ELEVEN

*The Park Plaza Hotel Bar*
*Boston, MA*

Corey let his eyes adjust to the dimly lit room. He found Devin sitting at a table towards the back.

He took off his overcoat, set it on a chair, then sat down to face Devin. It was a small table; Corey leaned in close. "What are you drinking?"

"Martini. Dry. What do you want?"

"The same. Extra olives."

"My, my, the young man grows up to big boy drinks."

"I'm not a kid anymore, Dev. I just turned eighteen. C'mon."

Devin swirled his martini glass on the sweat spot it left on the table. "What are you doing here, Corey?"

Corey smirked, "You told me to call, I called, so, here I am. What do you *think* I'm doing here?"

Devin sat forward. "Look, one drink and that's it. Tell me your story and that's it, okay?"

The waiter approached the table and Corey said, "Two more, make mine with extra olives, please."

The waiter bowed slightly, nodded, then went back to the bar.

Corey said, "Do you remember a cast party mom had, oh maybe five years ago at the house?"

"Your mom had lots of cast parties, Core."

"This was the one when you, Stu and Frank found your way up to my mother's dressing room and tried on some of her gowns. I think Frank was trying on every pair of her heels."

Devin smirked, "Oh, yeah. That one."

"Right. Well, I watched you guys. The whole time. I heard every word you said in there. I saw you kissing Stu, grabbing his crotch…the way you two looked at each other. It was the highlight of my night."

"I can only imagine. We were pretty tanked."

"No, you guys looked really good in mom's clothes. I remember going with her to buy those gowns."

"Oh, that's right, she took you clothes shopping with her. She told us you two were thick as thieves at Neiman Marcus. So, what's your point?"

"The point is, I knew back then that I was different. I had a mad crush on you. Remember how I watched you put your 'face' on for the shows? I was fascinated by everything you did."

"You had a crush on me…okay. So…?"

"I always wondered if I'd see you again. And here we are!"

The waiter returned with their drinks. Devin finished his first one then handed the empty glass to the waiter. "Okay, yes. Here we are. Corey, I'm almost eleven years older than you. What do you want from me?"

"What do you have to offer?"

Devin scowled. "Oh man…"

"Maybe you could show me the ropes in New York! I've already found my way to Christopher Street and all the local hangouts. I went to a GLF rally and met some pretty nice guys there. Maybe you could introduce me to a different crowd.":

"So, you want to get in with my crowd? I don't think so."

Corey reached under the table. "Oh, come on, Dev. What could be so bad about it?"

Devin jumped when Corey squeezed his thigh. "Jeez, Core!" He slipped his hand down under the table to meet Corey's. "You've become quite bold in your late teen hood!"

"Oh, I've been *bold* for a while now."

Devin leaned in. "Your mother knows you're a faggot."

"I prefer gay."

"She warned me last night, and in no uncertain terms, to not see you."

Corey took a long sip of his martini. "Hmph, must have seen the sparks fly."

"Corey, your mother is a good woman. She adores you, cares for you."

"I love her too, Devin, but she can't control my life."

"Look, I get that you're coming out of the closet—"

Corey smirked and shook his head. "You're a little late. I've been out of the closet since I was fifteen. Mom didn't find out until this summer."

"Oh, brother." Devin took a long sip of his drink. "I should just get up right now. This...this connection will be nothing but trouble."

"But you told me to call you. What was that all about?"

"Because you seemed like you needed an ally. But now I realize I can't be that ally for you."

Corey ignored the comment, reached back under the table, slid his torso closer to Devin and said, "No strings."

Devin drew his shoulders back. "Don't."

"One night. One fucking night."

Devin stilled Corey's hand under the table. "Why?"

"I promise to behave myself after this. I've fantasized about you for five years. It was divine intervention that brought you to CAP last night."

Devin sat still for a moment, fighting the desire between his legs. He looked at Corey, saw the glimmer in his dark eyes, the beautiful curve of his mouth, his sturdy chin, hair flopped over his forehead.

He signaled the waiter for the check, withdrawing his wallet and room key at the same time from his blazer pocket. "316. I'll be up shortly."

Corey downed his martini, scooted his chair back, grabbed the key and his overcoat, leaned down to Devin's ear and whispered, "You won't regret this."

Devin watched Corey exit the bar. He sighed, knew what he was about to do was wrong on so many levels; impulsive, stupid, *most* regretful, but...

He signed the check, collected his things, and made his way across the elegant lobby.

Corey was just a kid in a candy store.

Devin entered the elevator, pressed, '3' He remembered when he was Corey's age—every 'meeting' was a conquest, something to devour, an insatiable compulsion.

But he was a little older now, a bit more aware.

Still...

## Letters to Corey

## CHAPTER TWELVE

Corey went back to New York the Tuesday after Thanksgiving. The play at CAP closed with a sold-out final performance. All was copesetic at the Shapiro household until Risa bumped into Deborah's mother at the local market.

"Miriam! How are you?" Risa smiled.

Miriam smiled thinly, "Fine, Risa, and you?"

"Getting back to my normal routine after the holiday, the play, that kind of thing. I understand the kids got together over the weekend in Boston. How is Deborah doing at school."

"Got together?" She furrowed her eyebrows. "Who?"

Risa hesitated a moment then said, "Corey and Deborah."

"Not this weekend. Deborah was home with the flu."

Risa's smile faded. "What's that?"

"Deborah was home sick. And honestly, Risa, the *kids* are no longer an item."

Risa shook her head, "Wait a minute, what do you mean no longer an item?"

"Don't you know?"

"No, I don't. I thought they were, at least, friends!"

"Corey broke up with her a few weeks ago. Told her he needed to move on. She's devastated."

Risa looked off toward a woman squeezing lemons in the produce section. "I see."

"Doesn't Corey talk to you about these things?"

Risa murmured, "Well, of course there are things he does not share." She looked at Miriam, who was sizing her up. "I'm so sorry. I didn't know…"

"Well, maybe you should ask your son about it. He seems to have you all fooled. It's not my place to make assumptions, Risa. I don't know who he was meeting in Boston, but I can tell you it was *not* my daughter."

Risa tried to slow her heartbeat down. She could feel the color rise in her cheeks.

Forget secrets.

Now it included lies.

"I feel like a fool. I am so sorry."

Miriam turned her cart away from Risa. "Well, kids will be kids. She'll get over him, she's young enough to bounce back. They're both young enough to get over things. Take care, hello to Saul."

Risa nodded, standing still. "Sure thing. Say hi to Norman."

When Miriam was out of sight, Risa left her cart where it was and quickly exited the store. She slammed the car door after she got in, put her hands in the ten-and-two position on the steering wheel, then swore. "God*damn* it, Corey! *Why?*"

The first thing she did when she arrived home was to make an appointment with Alice. There was a cancellation for the following day.

She took it.

# CHAPTER THIRTEEN

*The Office of Alice Stern*

Risa paced instead of sitting down.

Alice watched then said gently, "I take it there are new developments."

"Oh, yes."

"Would you like to share?"

"I will. Yes." She finally sat down on the couch. "Things were going along so well, then…*bam*!"

"Does this have to do with Corey?"

"Yes, it does."

"Okay."

"So, I was recently in a play. After Thanksgiving, I reserved several seats for family and close friends. Corey had arrived home from New York the day before the holiday. We had a grand party after the show at the house. It was a terrific time. Do you remember me telling you about Devin, the young man I did several shows with years back?"

"Oh, yes, he was the person your son was enamored with."

"Yes, one and the same. Well, he was at the show. When he and Corey saw each other, there was an obvious connection between them. I never thought for a moment when I called Corey over to see him that…"

"That?"

She paused then said, "There would be sparks."

"Ah." Alice jotted some notes down on the pad and readjusted her glasses. "So, you saw the sparks fly, and then?"

"Long story short, Corey lied about where he was going the next day and with whom. He did not come home that night, claimed he missed the last train, would be spending the night with one of Deborah's friends at her apartment. I'm certain, now, that he was with Devin. Devin's in town with an off-Broadway troupe rehearsing for a show at the Orpheum."

"Okay, I see. Did Corey tell you about where he was going

before he left home?"

"He said he was going to see his girlfriend, Deborah, but…"

"He did not see her." Alice finished the sentence.

"That is correct." Risa nodded.

"How do you know this?"

"I ran into Deborah's mother at the market yesterday and she said not only did they *not* meet, but that Corey broke up with her a few weeks ago and that she was taking it pretty hard."

Alice nodded as she wrote. "Mm hmm. I assume Corey does not know you know."

"He does not."

"So, we've moved on from secrets now."

"Yes, to lies!"

"It would seem that way, yes."

Risa clasped her hands together over her knees. She shook her head. "I guess the out of sight out of mind way of thinking has backfired."

Alice said gently, "There is always that possibility, yes."

"Now what?" She looked directly at Alice.

"Now we break it down and decide how to move forward."

"Meaning?"

"It might be time to sit down with Corey and talk all this out. It's only going to get worse. I think you know that."

Risa blew out a breath and looked off. "I must tell you, Alice, I'm not happy about this at all. In fact, I'm very mad."

"I would think you would be."

Risa stood up and started to pace again, pumping her fist in the air in front of her. "How could he do this? I raised him to be *open* and *honest,* to *trust* me, to *know* he could come to me with *anything*!"

Again, Alice watched and waited until she sat back down. "Well, he *did* admit his activity to you."

Risa grunted, "Only because I *caught* him!"

"True."

Risa pursed her lips then said quietly. "Damn it all."

"Risa, this will work better if you can get ahold of your anger. It won't do you any good to make sense of this if you can't look at it objectively."

"How am I supposed to look at this objectively? This is my *son*. My flesh and *blood*!"

"Yes, he is. Try to remember he is experiencing something that is so much bigger than him. And perhaps the only way he can see his way through is to keep you thinking that everything is as normal as it could be."

"But it's *not*!"

"Is it possible he might be in some kind of denial of his own."

Risa took a deep breath and let it out. "Do you think *I'm* in denial?"

Alice chose her words carefully. "I think, perhaps, there is a certain amount of *understandable* denial in this case. This whole thing blindsided you and because of it, you feel forced into making decisions that might not be beneficial for either you, your son, or your husband. However," she set her pad and pen on the table. "I think you are starting to see *now* how secrets and lies can wear away the fabric of your familial relationships. Let's try to figure out a way to bring these to the surface. Would that be something we can do?"

"Well, we must do something, Alice. I can't take much more of this. I mean, what's next?" A sob caught in her throat. She snapped another tissue from the box and covered her face with it.

Alice said gently, "Then let's try to find a detour around a possible 'what is next' scenario."

*THERAPY NOTE:*
*Secrets and now lies, unraveling, anger/frustration, exponential escalation AS*

## CHAPTER FOURTEEN

*Manchester*
*December 1980*

The day before Corey was to arrive home for the two-week holiday break, Risa played out scenarios which she and Alice had discussed, promising not to let her anger override the importance of being as gentle as possible; to be loving yet *firm*; understanding that it was going to be about giving *Corey* a safe place to talk openly. Alice also directed her to be cautious about the possibility of Corey denying everything as well.

What she needed now was the truth.

*\*\*\**

The following day, Risa took the commuter rail into Boston's South Station where Corey's train was due to arrive from New York City at four-forty. Saul was going to meet them at their favorite Italian restaurant in Back Bay after work. But the train was delayed for almost an hour.

She waited at a café table in the atrium of the station, going over script requests for the next season at CAP, but her thoughts meandered. Instead, to calm her mind, she watched people bustle, listened to an announcer's sotto monotone voice call out arrivals and departures over the PA system. She imagined the station as if it were a stage with a George Gershwin or Cole Porter soundtrack; all the workers breaking into song and dance at specific moments. She mused, *what a fun show that would be—a major production!*

By six o'clock, the train finally pulled in from New York City. She gathered her things, went to a phone bank to call Saul, then joined the other people waiting for passengers at door 6. Steam coming from the hot wheels on the tracks coupled with the smell of diesel fuel and machine oil brought gusts of fetid, cold air each time the pneumatic doors opened letting passengers in.

When she saw Corey, her first thought was that he looked very tired. His normally bouncy gait was slow, shuffling. She moved forward to greet him. He smiled but it wasn't the smile she knew. It looked forced. His color was not good. She hoped he wasn't coming down with something.

He approached her. "Hi, mom!" He let go of his rolling suitcase handle.

She put her arms around him, brought him close. "Hi, son."

He clung to her. "I'm so glad to finally be here. What a nightmare ride."

"Oh, honey, you must be famished."

He pulled back from her. "Am I ever! I had a flimsy sandwich at Penn Station. Ugh."

She brushed his bangs from his forehead, taking a quick inventory. His eyes did not sparkle, his skin looked mottled. She asked with a fair amount of concern in her voice, "Are you feeling okay?"

"Just tired. A long week of tests."

"Well, I talked to your dad, he's going to meet us at Restani's for dinner. Are you up for it?"

"I can taste the fresh bread as we speak."

She looped her arm through his. "Let's get a cab."

On the short ride through city traffic to Back Bay, Risa held his hand. He was unusually quiet. A shiver ran down her spine. She made a few attempts at general conversation regarding school; his answers were brief.

Once at the restaurant, Corey excused himself to go to the lavatory.

Saul stopped at the coatroom then joined Risa at their table. He kissed her then sat down. "I assume Corey is indisposed?"

"He is."

"How was your day?"

"Saul, Corey doesn't look right."

"What do mean he doesn't look right?"

"Tired. Not himself."

"Well, he just got off from a delayed train. And mid-terms. Tough stuff, Reese, I would understand that."

"I can't put my finger on it. Just something a mother knows."

Saul took her hand. "Now honey."

Corey came around the back of his father and hugged him. "Hey, Dad!"

"Son! Let me look at you!"

Corey sat down in the empty chair between his parents. Saul asked while looking him over, "How are you?"

"Exhausted, really. But otherwise, fine."

Saul gently clapped his hand on Corey's shoulder. "Perfectly understandable. Let's get some decent food into your belly. You'll feel better."

Mid-way through dinner, Corey excused himself to go to the lavatory again. As soon as he was out of earshot, Saul leaned in toward Risa. "I'm going to have to agree with you. Something is not quite right."

Risa put her fork down, suddenly not hungry. "Do you think I should make an appointment with Walt Berkowitz?"

"Let's just see how he feels tomorrow."

When Corey returned to the table, he looked better. "Sorry, I guess that nasty sandwich at Penn Station didn't agree with me at all."

Risa took his hand. "Let's go home. We can take all this to go, okay? Dad drove in, you can rest in the car."

"Yes, let's. I'll be better tomorrow. I haven't had much sleep of late."

***

Corey slept until noon the next day. Risa busied herself in the kitchen, the den, the living room. She sent Saul and Rachel on errands.

She heard Corey upstairs shuffle from his room to the bathroom. She waited for him at the bottom of the steps.

"Hi, mom!" He had more pep in his step as he made his way down to her.

"Hi, son! Feeling better?"
"Like a new man. What's for breakfast?"
"Lunch?"
"Both!" He hugged her.
She felt his ribs through his robe. "You slept well, then?"
"Like a dead man."
"Don't even kid about that! C'mon, I've got a whole spread set up for you."
They walked arm in arm into the kitchen. "Deal me in. I could use a little coffee."
"Fresh pot, son."
Risa whipped up eggs with ham, onion, tomato, basil, and spinach. She set two large pieces of fresh French bread in the toaster, poured fresh-squeezed orange juice, then sat down opposite him with her own coffee mug, pleased to see him happily eating. He was back to himself. All he needed was a good night's sleep.
Corey asked, "What's your plan for today?"
"Nothing special. Maybe you and I could take a drive to the beach, bundle up, walk the surf's edge like we used to? Only if you feel up to it."
He ate steadily, nodded. "I would like that."

***

After they made their way down to the hard-packed sand, and walked a bit, Risa told herself it was now or never. She took a deep breath, stopped, and faced him, taking his hands in hers. "Son, I need to talk to you about something."
"Okay."
"I need you to be perfectly honest with me because…well…it's the only way."
"Okay."
"Corey, I need to know if you are gay."
He tilted his head to the side, frowned, snorted. "Hmph. Nothing like coming right out and asking."
"It's a legitimate question that deserves an honest answer."

He looked down at his feet. When he brought his gaze back to her, he said quietly, "Yes."

She nodded. A jet plane flew over on its approach to Logan Airport. They waited for it to disappear before regarding one another after his admission.

Risa felt a rush of relief coupled with despair regarding the raw truth of the situation. She felt heady. They looked at one another for a moment then Corey disengaged his hands from hers and shoved them deep into his coat pockets. He turned to face the ocean. "What gave me away?"

"Well, for one thing, your lies. I ran into Deborah's mother a few weeks ago at the market. She informed me that you and Deborah weren't even speaking to one another. The day you claimed to be meeting her in town, she was down with the flu. And when you did not return home that evening, I felt it in my bones: you were with Devin, weren't you?"

"Mom, I—"

She turned him gently by the shoulders to face her again. "Look Corey, maybe I really don't want to know the details. Your life is your own. When you are away from home, you live your life as you see fit. However, when you are here, at home, you live by our standards."

He nodded, his eyes clouding over. "Mom, I never…"

"Corey, no more lies, at least, with me. Because right now I am your only ally in this situation."

"What about dad?"

"It's up to you to speak with him. It can't come from me."

Corey shivered, sighed, then turned away from her. "This is so fucked up. Are you disappointed in me?"

"I'm not disappointed. I'm sure you are doing the best you can. This cannot be easy on you." She looped her arm through his and held him close. She felt for him, knew he struggled. After all that she and Alice discussed, how could he not?

"It's not. I don't even understand it myself. Sometimes I don't know where I fit in. I try to be the all-around cool guy but then everyone has all these expectations. Like, some of the girls in the dorm want to date me. Even a few guys have shown interest on the sly. I feel like an island."

Risa felt a deep sadness settle in her heart. How could she answer him? "Oh, honey, of *course!* People want to get close to you! You're smart, funny, sweet, attractive. And you're just starting out in life. So…vulnerable." She felt her throat close, tears threatening. "All I can do is love you. You will find your way through this, I am certain."

Corey stopped walking, turned his mother to face him and pulled her into his arms. She clung to the lapels of his overcoat, closing her eyes against the inevitable sob that escaped her throat.

Life continued to move around them: planes landed, the tide shuffled shells onto the water's edge, children played further down the beach, dogs ran for sticks. Couples walked hand in hand.

They stood like that, mother, and son, in an embrace that felt to Risa like the end of one life and the unstable, unpredictable beginning of another.

It had been a long six months.

# CHAPTER FIFTEEN

***Thursday June 25, 1981***
***The Following Year***

The phone rang at six thirty in the evening.

Risa covered the pot with the spaghetti sauce cooking and turned down the heat as she picked up the receiver, cradling it between her shoulder and her ear. "Hello?"

"Hello, is this Mrs. Risa Shapiro?" A gentle-voiced Asian accented woman asked.

"It is! Who is calling?"

"My name is Doctor Leona Wong. I am a specialist at the Memorial Sloan Kettering Hospital in New York City. Would your husband, Saul Shapiro, be home?"

"He is." She looked out the kitchen bay window at Saul, who was reeling in the garden hose after watering all the plants in the yard. "We've already donated this year. What is this about?"

"It is something of a delicate nature, it would probably be best to speak with both of you at this time."

Risa's mood went from light and airy to concern. "Does this have to do with our son, Corey?"

"It would be best if I could talk to you both. Would that be possible right now?"

Risa went to the window, knocked on the glass with her knuckles. Saul turned, she pointed to the phone, motioned him indoors. He was about to wave her off but must have seen the look on her face. He dropped the hose, came into the house through the back sliding door off the patio. He mouthed, "Who is it?"

Risa covered the mouthpiece with her hand, murmured, "Pick up the extension in your office. It's from New York."

It took him only moments to reach his desk. "Hello, this is Saul Shapiro, who is this?"

"Oh, good evening Mr. Shapiro, this is Doctor Leona Wong

from Memorial Sloan Kettering Hospital in New York. I'm calling today to inform you of some news regarding your son."

Risa held her breath as Saul inquired, "And what might that be, Doctor Wong?"

She cleared her throat. "Well, there is no good way to say this. Your son is ill. He is in a private ward right now. We believe this is something of an immune deficiency issue."

Risa's insides trembled as Saul pursued the questioning. "Something of an immune deficiency issue? Please explain further."

"Well, I think it would be best if you were both able to come to New York to meet with me."

Risa blurted out, "Is it that bad? I want to see my son!"

"I can certainly understand that Mrs. Shapiro." The doctor's voice was calm, gentle, but with urgency. "And you will, but first, we must a have a conversation so I can share the details of his condition with you."

Risa's voice was choked, "What condition are you talking about? When did he get sick? Are you sure you have the right family?" Risa knew she was grabbing at straws. "I mean, *really*, doctor!"

Saul interrupted, "Can you be more specific, Doctor Wong? This comes as quite a shock, as you can well imagine."

The lid on the pot with the spaghetti sauce started to rumble. Risa went to the stove and snapped off the heat.

"Yes, I can, Mr. Shapiro. But as I said, it would be best if both of you could come to New York to meet with me."

Risa picked up a dishrag, wiped an already dry countertop with it. "I'm confused. What is wrong with our son?" she asked.

"Are you both aware of the term HIV."

Risa nodded, closed her eyes, speechless. HIV was all over the news. She blatantly ignored it, not wanting to think for even one second that Corey could *possibly*—

Saul said guardedly, "Yes, we've been hearing about it. What does that have to do with our son? This thing is being hailed as the gay plague."

Risa held her breath as the silence from the other end of the phone was broken with Saul stating, "Well, this has nothing to do with our son. He is *not* a homosexual."

Dr. Wong took a deep breath. "This is complicated, Mr. and Mrs. Shapiro. I think—"

Saul cut her off. "Listen, Doctor Wong, what does this *gay plague have to do with our son*?"

Another silence.

Risa found her voice. "When should we come to see you?"

"Tomorrow would be best."

Saul began to protest, "Tomorrow? I can't just—"

"We will be there," Risa cut him off.

The doctor said, "Good, let me give you my direct phone number. Call me when you arrive in town. If I am not there to answer, the service will page me."

Risa wrote the information down with a shaky hand. "Thank you, Doctor, we will see you tomorrow." She hung up the extension, closed her eyes and willed time to retract the last ten minutes of her life.

She heard Saul say goodbye to the doctor then listened as he neared the kitchen, her heartbeat increasing with each footfall. There was no way she could, or would, lie her way out of this. The time had come to reveal her burden.

When he entered the room, he asked, "What is going on here, Risa?"

She swallowed around the dryness in her throat. "Saul, we need to talk."

Risa watched his face morph right in front of her eyes: his nose appeared bigger, mouth pinched, eyes sunk deeper into their sockets. After what felt like several minutes, but was only seconds, he said, "So, talk."

She tried to collect herself. "Let's go sit in the living room?"

He made no move toward the living room. "Is our son a homosexual?"

"Saul, it's—"

"*Is our son a homosexual*?" He said through clenched teeth.

"Yes." She held her breath.

He nodded, turned his face toward the stove as if someone were standing right there. "Well, what do you know, I have a *faggola* for a son."

"Please don't call him that, it's demeaning."

Saul snapped his head back in her direction. "And I suppose having sex with another man is *not* demeaning? Tell me, how long have you known?"

She looked away. "Since last summer."

He regarded her by shaking his head, then nodded to this unseen person. "You see? Since last summer!"

"Saul, Corey is in trouble right now, we need to focus on that."

"I need facts, Risa. *Facts*! Did he tell you he was a homosexual, or did you find out somehow?"

"I…came upon him in the woods behind the house with another boy."

"Behind the house. Well, I'll give him a gold star for *daring*. Did you do anything to stop it? Confront them?"

"No. I was in shock. I spoke to him the next day. He promised me it wouldn't happen again. But…"

"But…*what*?"

"I felt it was not over."

"And yet you did not talk to me about it." He snorted. "So, you had a mother's intuition?"

"Yes, I did."

"What do you think of a mother who takes her son into a ladies' dressing room with her when he is nine years old? What do you think of a mother who brings her very impressionable eleven-year-old son to the theatre with her, exposing him to all her *faggola* cast mates?"

Risa was aghast at his bitterness. "Saul! How *dare* you!"

"Well? What *do* you think?"

"Don't you *ever*!"

In his alarmingly passive court voice he continued, "You kept this from me for more than a year. Why?"

She had no answer. He was right. She had betrayed him in the worst possible way. "I did it for Corey."

"You did it for Corey," he repeated. "So, you lied to *me* to protect *him*, is that correct, Risa?"

Risa faced him head-on. "Yes! I did! I knew it was wrong,

but I was terrified for him."

"Terrified? Aren't you being a bit dramatic? Oh, wait, that's right, you're an actress."

Risa looked away from him, floored that he would throw this in her face. When she brought her gaze back up, she said quietly, "And how about *you* tell *me* how you would have reacted to your son? Tell me that, Saul! How would you have taken the news that he was gay?" She folded her arms across her chest, started to pace, her nerves teetering on the edge. "We *all* know how Saul Shapiro feels about those men who are," she made quotation marks with her fingers in the air, "light in the loafers, queers, fairies. He hates them, is *reviled* by them, he thinks they are less-than, a black mark on society."

He shook his head turning his back to her. "Don't make yourself out to be the victim, Risa. You are the one who withheld crucial information."

She stepped around him, faced him again. "Crucial information, Saul? This isn't a *goddamned* courtroom! Can you at least tell me why you have such hatred for gay people?"

"I can't, Risa."

She searched for a reaction in his eyes; they were almost blank. She asked him gently, "Saul, did something happen to you when you were younger?"

"Why would you ask that?"

"Because there has to be *something*, a reason why you feel the way you do."

"Can't a man just have his opinions?"

"An opinion is one thing, but if there is something deeper than that, then what?"

He steadied himself on the counter and cut her off. "Not *now*!"

She drew back. It took her a moment to recover from the sting of his delivery.

He shifted the conversation, "Curious, Risa. Who have you been sharing this with over the last year? Peg? Your mother? Does everyone know about this but me?"

Risa lifted her chin. "No one knows. Saul, I've been…talking to a therapist."

He cocked his head, his eyebrows raised. "A therapist." Again, he faced the unseen figure at the stove. "Let's add this to the mix, shall we? A therapist! Right under my nose! She's been talking to a *complete stranger*!" He turned to face her. "And does this therapist condone the secrecy from your husband?"

"No, she does not. But it's not her place to tell me what to do. She only offers guidance for how I feel."

"So, you're talking to someone who doesn't guide you to do the right thing, but gives you the green light to lie, a shoulder to cry on, an audience?"

Risa sighed heavily. "Enough with the acting comments. It's more in-depth than a shoulder to cry on, Saul. I don't think you understand."

He shook his head.

"Saul, listen. Can't we talk about this later? Right now, we must focus on getting to New York to see Corey and sort out his medical issues immediately."

He withdrew his wallet from a back pocket, pulled a credit card from the slot. "Go ahead and make the arrangements. I need to go for a drive."

"Saul."

He grabbed his keys from the hook on the wall near the door. "I'll be back later."

Risa continued to watch after he had slammed the door behind him. The sound reverberated in the all-too quiet house. She leaned against the counter near the sink until she heard Saul start his car then gun the engine down the driveway.

Then her legs gave way and she dropped to the floor, a wail erupting from her chest. She screamed into the empty house; her tears relentless as the year of pent-up emotions found their way out. Rocking, holding herself around her midsection, she cried like a baby.

When she finally composed herself, she stood up and leaned over the sink to rinse her face with cold water. As she looked out the window to their beautifully landscaped backyard, she chuckled mirthlessly. It didn't even feel like the same day, the same life; they had just returned from Maui where they spent their 25th wedding anniversary, Rachel was away at summer camp in the Berkshires as a junior counselor, Corey was in summer session at school.

Life was as perfect and carefree as it could be.

And this evening had started like so many others before it; Saul arrived home at five-thirty to change his clothes and tend to the gardens. Risa started the spaghetti sauce, tossed a salad, sliced fresh bread, and popped the cork on a bottle of Pinot Grigio. It was going to be another gorgeous June evening; they would eat outside under the umbrella on the terrace, then go for ice-cream at the beach, take a walk at the water's edge to watch the moon rise over the bay.

Glorious.

But then the call.

As if on cue, Risa snapped out of her dark moment and opened the Yellow Pages for the Eastern Airlines number. While she waited for an agent, she wished she could take back the year of deceit. If she had only been forthcoming with Saul regarding Corey, perhaps this whole thing might not have happened. Perhaps Saul would insist that Corey not go to school in New York City. Perhaps right now, Corey would not be sick with something called the gay plague. For a moment she stood paralyzed with the receiver slipping from her ear: if she had just been up front with Saul maybe Corey would not be—

"Thank you for holding, this is Claudette, how may I help you today?."

"Yes, I would like to book a flight for my husband and I to New York City."

*Secrets reveal themselves when we least expect…you had to make a choice at the time that you thought was right.*

On autopilot, Risa made the reservations, called the hotel where they were elite guest members and booked a room, then went about cleaning up the kitchen, transferring the sauce into a container for the freezer, loading the dishwasher and making sure the countertops were clean and dry.

\*\*\*

The jet to La Guardia bounced through obese gray rain

clouds. By the time they made it to the hospital, Risa's stomach was in knots.

Doctor Leona Wong introduced herself to Risa and Saul in the lobby of Memorial Sloan Kettering. Risa immediately liked her kind, soft brown eyes, feeling the doctor's professionalism from a gentle but firm handshake.

The doctor quietly intoned, "Please, let's go up to my office where we can speak privately."

Her office was spartan with just the right appointments for efficiency. The muted colors helped Risa to relax—as much as she could under the circumstances.

Dr. Wong said, "Please, have a seat." Showing them to two armchairs in front of her desk. She went around and sat down at her desk and opened a folder. "Thank you for coming today on such short notice. I realize this is a difficult situation so I will be as thorough as I can and answer any questions you will have." She slipped on a pair of small round glasses then cleared her throat. "Two days ago, your son presented at the campus health center with symptoms of a pneumonia-like flu: headache, fever, nausea, vomiting, and labored breathing. Upon examination while listening to his lungs, they found three small dark lesions on the skin of his back. They treated him initially for dehydration with IV fluids which he tolerated very well. He was then sent, by ambulance, to our emergency ward here where I first met him. Upon examination, we immediately called for bloodwork panels, and treated him with Albuterol Sulfate for his labored breathing and started an IV of antibiotics. I was most concerned with his breathing and the lesions. You see, with HIV, there are tell-tale signs that must be evaluated without delay. And I felt your son needed to be evaluated immediately."

Saul asked, "Just what is HIV?"

"HIV stands for Human Immunodeficiency Virus. This is a very new virus that researchers across the country are scrambling to understand. So, let me break it down for you as best I can. Our immune system is a biological process which protects us against disease. It responds to and detects a wide variety of agents, which could be a virus, a parasite, things of that nature. Basically, a healthy immune system will distinguish these pathogens from our healthy cells and tissues to fight them off, keep things in cheque. So, in the case of the HIV process, a virus enters the bloodstream and attaches to certain cells. Flu-like symptoms occur during the acute infection stage. Now, this can last for up to two weeks, then the person starts to feel better, nothing more to seek medical attention for. Meanwhile, the virus is still at work as it travels to the lymph nodes, replicates rapidly in the absence of antibodies which can take one to three months to produce. Are you still with me?"

Risa and Saul nodded.

"There is a process called subversion, which in general terms can be explained best this way: after the body has begun to produce antibodies to combat a certain virus—in this case HIV—the immune system gradually loses the battle. And, of course," she sighed, "we are still researching this process. It is very involved. Now, let us discuss T cells. T cells, or CD4 cells, are integral in fighting off infection. They become depleted. This could take years, but we are finding that T-cell depletion could take much less time. Your son has enlarged lymph nodes over most of his body. The blood tests should be back later today."

Saul leaned forward and asked, "So, you suspect this HIV is what is happening to our son? You said something about lesions on his back?"

"Yes, this is what initially alerted us to take this course of action. You see, we have most recently added another type of problem we have been seeing now. Kaposi Sarcoma is a cancer that develops from the cells that line lymph nodes and blood vessels. In this case, we are looking carefully at the lymph involvement. Now, not to confuse the issue, but Kaposi is generally found in older men, but with HIV, we are finding it in much younger men."

Risa interjected. "Wait a moment, you said cancer?"

"Yes. It is a complicated process. In people diagnosed with HIV, the added component is demonstrated by the presence of Kaposi in the lungs. So, in essence, it is one bad set of cells invading good cells and causing the losing battle I spoke of just a few moments ago."

Saul said, "So, in essence, our son has cancer."

Doctor Wong raised her forefinger. "Well, not exactly. The HIV was introduced into his body, and it was the progression to the Kaposi component that brings the cancerous cells to the forefront."

He asked, "How was it introduced into his body?"

"One of the ways is sexual intercourse with an infected individual. Which brings me to Corey's history. He told me about both of you, about his sister, that you've not had any major illnesses in the family that he knew of."

Risa nodded, "That is correct."

"I asked him if he had had any flu-like symptoms in the last five months, like the ones he presented with initially at the health center. He reported that he'd had a bout with something back in April."

Risa sat forward, "Yes. I coached him from home how to take care of himself. I was ready to fly down, but he told me he had some friends taking care of him. And," she added, "he told me not to worry. I was concerned about his cough, however."

Doctor Wong nodded. "Yes, this would be consistent with the progression." She leaned forward now, not referring to notes. "I had to ask him questions of a personal nature regarding his sexual experiences. As I said, HIV is transmitted via mucosal contact. Also, from the use of a shared drug needle, or extremely poor environmental conditions. I ruled out the last two given his familial history. Corey was reticent at first but after I explained the importance to be forthcoming, he went on to share that he'd had many encounters with men."

Saul murmured, "Many." He shook his head, looking somewhere over Doctor Wong's shoulder. "I suppose he was in the right place at the right time to catch this thing, correct?" He looked back at the doctor.

Risa said, barely above a whisper, "More like the wrong place at the wrong time."

The doctor nodded, "Yes, and unfortunately with widespread contact, we have no way of finding these people. In a perfect world we would try to get the names and addresses of his partners."

The word *promiscuity* came to Risa's mind. Her intuition

that Corey had been practicing this lifestyle long before she caught him last summer…she pushed the thoughts back down and asked quietly, "Is there a cure?"

Doctor Wong hesitated for a moment, took off her glasses and folded them neatly on her desk blotter. "Sadly, as of right now, there are no cures. Only medications, treatment therapies, will hopefully slow the process down thereby keeping the T-cell count as high as possible. As I said, the T-cells help to fight the infection. You must understand that this is a relatively new virus, we are trying to make sense of all the data."

Risa put her head in her hands, closed her eyes, and said quietly, "I need to use the restroom."

"Of course. If you go left from my office door, it will be on the right across the hall."

Risa shakily rose from the chair, steadied herself then walked out of the office.

Thankfully, the bathroom was empty when she entered. She ran to the first toilet and wretched. She held onto the seat, feeling another round of nausea in the form of *cancer, no cure, hopeful drug therapies,* sweep from her gut.

When there was nothing left to bring up, she flushed the toilet, sat back on her haunches, took a few deep breaths, then stood, and straightened her clothes. At the sink mirror, her reflection showed red-rimmed and dull eyes; dull from the information imparted over the last half an hour.

Her mouth felt like a sock of sand.

When she arrived back at Dr. Wong's office, Saul was not in his chair. She reached into her purse, worked a piece of chewing gum from the pack and folded it into her mouth.

"Can I get you anything, Mrs. Shapiro? I'm concerned."

She thought, *you should be.* "Maybe some water, or perhaps you have a Coca-Cola? I haven't eaten much; the flight was bumpy. I think I need either caffeine or sugar right now. Both would be best."

"I understand." Dr. Wong stood and walked over to a mini fridge, extracted a can of Coke, and pulled two glasses from a shelf above. "Our cafeteria is quite good. I suggest something to eat before seeing your son." She poured an equal amount of soda into the glasses.

"After." Risa gladly sipped at first then took a long pull. The carbonation felt good going down her parched throat. "Doctor, I know you are being very diplomatic with us, explaining everything you can. My husband did not know about Corey's proclivity before last night." She almost divulged how ugly the conversation was, how little they had spoken since then.

"I know. Corey informed me. He is quite nervous about seeing his father today. He begged me not to say anything, but…under the circumstances, there was no other choice."

*Secrets reveal themselves at the precise time…*

"When can we see him?"

"There are a few more things we should go over before you see him."

Saul returned to the office. He set his hand on Risa's shoulder. "Are you okay?"

"Not really. The Coke is helping, though."

Saul reached for his glass. He regarded the doctor. "Anything stronger?"

She chuckled, "Not right now, but perhaps later you will."

"Please, go on."

"At this time, Corey is not in advanced stages of HIV, however because his immune system has been compromised, he is in our quarantine ward. Also, and this is somewhat maddening—it must be—he will most likely have to stop attending school. I had to report this to the Dean of Students, a mister Walden Newton, at the university—as proscribed by the CDC. The Dean is expecting your call later today. Here is the number." She handed the slip of paper to Saul.

Risa breathed deeply through her nose to quell another round of nausea building. "Oh, God." She looked at Saul. "Not go back to school?"

"You mentioned that he was in quarantine. Is what he has communicable?" Saul inquired as he folded the piece of paper with Walden Newton's phone number on it and murmured to Risa, "We will clear this up later today."

"No, not by breathing the same air or touching him. He is quarantined for his own protection. Until we regulate his T-cells, the environment must be as germ free as possible. If you don't accidentally stick yourself with the same needle used to start his IV, or to draw blood from, you are not at risk."

Risa leaned forward. "Please, I just want to see my son. Can we do that now?"

"Yes, I will take you to him. You will have to don mask, gloves, and gown before entering his room."

Risa stood up. "I don't care if I have to don Viking Armor. I just need to see him right now."

They rode the elevator to the eleventh floor, or 'Q' ward as intoned by the doctor, in silence. The Ward was eerily quiet, all the patient doors were closed with certain types of equipment outside their rooms. The activity at the nurse's station, directly in front of the elevator bank, reminded Risa of a fish tank: medical personnel moving around each other in orchestrated precision. The noise was contained to shoes squeaking on high-glossed linoleum floors, intermittent beeps from overhead monitor screens showing real-time patient vital stats, and hushed speaking voices. There was no bustle, ringing phones, or idle chit-chat.

Doctor Wong approached the desk, took Corey's chart from the rack, then led Risa and Saul down the hall to his room, where a rolling cart with clean sterile wear stood just outside the door. The doctor gowned up first, knocked on the door, then donned gloves. She entered the room after a few moments, closing the door behind her with her foot.

Risa and Saul helped each other with the clothing. When the doctor re-emerged from Corey's room, she said, "He is awake and ready to see you."

Risa nodded, her heart trip-hammering in her chest. She could feel her pulse bound through her inner ears as she stepped toward the door. Using her shoulder to open it, as the doctor demonstrated, she gave it a push.

She did not know what to expect but when she saw her son at first glance, he looked physically normal—save for the oxygen mask fitted around his nose and mouth and the IV line rigged to his arm.

She quickly went to him, bent down awkwardly in her

required garb, tried to avoid the oxygen mask, and took his head into her hands to look at him. "Oh, son."

Corey threw his arms around her waist, leaning into her, "Mommy…" he started to cry, as did Risa. She knew she was supposed to keep him calm but there was nothing on God's green earth that could stop the run-away train from careening dead center into her heart.

Saul stepped up, put his hand on Corey's arm, held on. "Son, I'm here. We will figure this whole thing out."

Corey howled into his mother's chest, the oxygen mask now askew on his face.

As she ran her gloved hands around his head, clinging to his hair, she became aware of the weight of it lodged into the hollow of her solar plexus, and knew at once that she would bear an indissoluble strength.

For herself.

For her family.

For the rest of his life.

## CHAPTER SIXTEEN

*New York City*
*St. James Hotel*
*Same Day*

Risa said to Saul, "What are we going to tell the family? More to the point, yours."

His eyes darkened. "I don't know yet."

"Saul, we need to tell them something."

"Let's think this out carefully, Risa. There is a lot at stake."

"At stake? This is our son we're talking about."

"I realize that. I think we need to do this methodically. Bringing this news and all that goes with it is going to be tricky, wouldn't you agree?"

"I would, but from what Doctor Wong says, this is not going to clear up anytime soon."

"We keep it simple, that he has a rare lung affliction."

Risa shook her head slowly. "I don't know. I suppose that will suffice for now. I can't make any promises with my mom and dad."

They sat across from each other at the hotel café, the food on their plates half-eaten. She put her fork down and looked away from her husband. "I am sorry I withheld information from you, Saul. It wasn't right. It was like carrying a ten-ton weight. Maybe if I had been more forthcoming, more confident with..."

He folded his napkin and tucked it underneath his plate. "You don't have to explain any further. It happened; it is what it is. The shock has been replaced with a dire situation. But let's keep this in perspective. We must figure out what our next moves are going to be." He reached into his inner jacket pocket and withdrew the phone number for Walden Newton. "Let's start here, with Mr. Newton. Then we can decide the next course of action."

Risa allowed her husband to take the reins. She was so tired, so deflated.

***

Risa disliked Walden Newton immediately. He had an odor about him—something old and dirty camouflaged by a pungent men's cologne. His attempts as a long-haired, scruffy-faced hipster came off as just plain disheveled. It was not at all what she would have thought the Dean of Students at a prestigious school should look like.

After he ushered them into his office, he closed the door and sat down at his oversized desk strewn with papers and file folders. He cleared his throat and began. "We have a difficult situation here. There is no easy way to go about this. After speaking with the experts at Memorial, it has been decided that Corey will not be able to return to school from here on in. His...*condition* prohibits him from rejoining the general population. As you can well see, my main concern is the student body." He pulled an envelope from a file folder. "Now, we have already packed his belongings into boxes. They are in a storage unit in mid-town. I have the key and address right here for you."

Saul shot forward. "You *what*?"

Risa was aghast.

Walden lifted his hand, palm side out toward them. "The CDC instructed us to remove his belongings from his room. We follow the rules."

Saul leaned in. "I'm at a loss here, Walden. Why would they instruct you to do that? What Corey has is not communicable in that way—as I am *sure* Doctor Wong explained to you. I am a lawyer and frankly, what you have done is against the law."

"I can appreciate your position, sir, but the CDC sets the precedence. Your fight is with them. As you can well imagine, this new virus is..." he stopped himself. "We cannot take any chances with the volume of students at this school, let alone at the residence hall."

Risa shook her head slowly and looked at Saul. "I can't believe this."

Saul lowered his voice.. "So, let me get this straight. You handled all our son's belongings—did you wear protective clothing? Boxed them up, then sent them to a storage unit?"

Walden did not answer him about the protective clothing. "We had to. It was out of our hands by then."

Saul stood abruptly, towering over Walden and the shipwreck of a desk. "Give me the key. And I want a copy of his school records and anything else that might be on file for him."

Walton ruffled papers around. "Yes, well, I can certainly get that information to you by the end of next week. It's going to take a bit of time."

Saul now leaned in. "Oh, really, as much time as, say, it took for you to clear out his belongings? I want those papers delivered to the hotel we are staying at by the end of business *tomorrow*!"

Walden nodded slowly. "I can certainly appreciate your anger but—"

Risa suddenly rose from her chair. "But *nothing*! I can see how *dedicated* you are to the student body, Mister Newton, but from where I sit, your bedside manners are simply deplorable. We are talking about a young man here. You might just want to *learn* more about this *condition* that you so speak of. I have a feeling you will be seeing more of it in the very near future." She turned to open the office door but pivoted before reaching the doorknob. "It's called HIV and I'm certain Corey is not the only one in a residence hall of six hundred who is infected."

Saul followed his wife. "The paperwork, Mister Newton, at the St. James Hotel in Manhattan. By five o'clock. *Tomorrow!*"

## CHAPTER SEVENTEEN

*The St. James Hotel*
*New York City*
*Friday August 21, 1981*

When Risa woke the next morning from a fitful sleep, she had no idea where she was for a moment. She reached over to the other side of the bed, found it empty, then sat up. "Saul?"

The room was eerily quiet. She heard muffled screeching tires, honking horns, and big trucks rumbling through intersections on the streets below through the hermetically sealed windows from their fifteenth-floor suite. Just another normal day in the city that never sleeps.

When she realized Saul was not in the room, she stood up, stretched, then went into the bathroom. Her reflection made her wince. She turned away.

Her mind reeled. The last twenty-four hours were a blur. What she wanted more than anything was to be with her son but visiting hours didn't start until noon. It had been hard enough to leave him the night before, as he seemed a bit better; and while his color was off, his mood and spirit were more in the line of *'get me the hell out of here'*.

She and Saul had discussed their next move over dinner at the hospital after their visit with Walden Newton. While it was strongly recommended that Corey remain hospitalized, Saul and Risa wanted him closer to home. The doctor assured them that she would contact her colleagues at the Massachusetts General Hospital in Boston to see if a bed would be available for him within the week.

She went to the phone next to the bed and picked up the receiver. Her nerves were on edge, and she hoped Saul was out getting them coffee and something to eat.

Her first call was to schedule an appointment with Alice for the following week in hopes they would be back to Boston by then.

The next call was person-to-person.

When Ruthie answered, Risa could not hold back the tears. She had so much to say and no idea where to start. She said with a trembling voice, "Mom..."

"Risa! What is it, honey?"

"I have something to tell you."

Ruthie called out to Abe, "Get on the extension, Abe. It's Risa. Something is wrong."

Abe picked up the extension quickly. "Okay, honey. I'm here."

"Saul and I are in New York City. Corey is...in the hospital."

"Corey is ill?" Abe asked.

"Yes, he has a...oh God."

Ruthie kept the alarm out of her voice, "What, honey. What does Corey have?"

She took a deep breath. "He has a rare lung affliction."

"A rare lung affliction? What does this mean?" Ruthie asked.

"The doctors are running tests now. They've got him on oxygen and IV drip medications. He's in good hands."

Ruthie asked, "How did he get sick? When did this happen?"

Risa felt the urge to hang up, run; the lie came too easily. But the nagging truth underneath the lie tore at her. There was no running, not from this, not from her loving parents. She said matter-of-factly, "Mom, dad, he has HIV."

The silence on the other end of the phone was palpable. Risa closed her eyes and whispered, "Oh, God."

Ruthie asked gently, "Can you bring him home?"

"Yes, the doctor here is trying to get him a bed at Mass General."

Abe asked, "What does this mean, HIV?"

Ruthie said to Abe, "Let's you and I discuss this later. Right now, Risa needs us."

Through a raw throat, Risa resigned. "Yes, I do."

# CHAPTER EIGHTEEN

*The Office of Alice Stern*
*Friday July 3, 1981*

Alice waited.
Risa composed herself.
Alice said, "I am so sorry, Risa. I'm glad you're here."
"I can't even tell you. It's been a week from hell."
"I'm sure it was. Take your time."
Risa sat back and closed her eyes. "Saul is taking this much better than I thought he would. As always, the pragmatic one in the family. He sees everything in facts and results."
"And you? How are you taking all this?"
"It feels like I'm on one of those spin rides, where the walls move so fast you don't even know you're moving."
Alice chuckled, "Ah, yes, the centrifugal ride."
"Well, if I could turn back the hands of time."
Alice nodded. "So, I gather that Corey is in good hands at MGH?"
"Yes, I like his doctor. His name is Chaim Nori. He has colleagues in San Francisco who are working day and night to research the virus. He promised me he is going to fight like hell to get Corey back on his feet."
"I'm sure this sets your mind at ease." Alice jotted a few notes down.
"It does."
"So, let's go back to the night in question when you received the phone call from Memorial. Aside from the obvious concerns Saul would have about Corey, how did he take the news about Corey's lifestyle?"
"Not well. He blamed me for certain things, I blamed him for his hatred of gay men. It went around in circles with him leaving the house to go for a drive. What is it about men who must leave the house to go for a drive when they are upset?"

"Probably for the same reason we women go shopping when we're upset."

Risa sighed. "Oh Alice…you are so right about that!"

"So, how does it feel to have the secret out in the open now?"

"It feels right. But I'm still stymied as to Saul's reticence. I feel that something must have happened to him at some point in time."

"A gut feeling?"

"Yes. And if I am being honest here, my gut feelings have been falling right into place, haven't they? When Corey was home last year, something didn't seem quite right. And now that I've talked with Doctor Wong and Doctor Nori, they both concur that Corey may have been initially sick at that time. That the virus has taken this long to rear its ugly head."

Alice asked, "Have you shared this news with Rachel yet?"

"She comes home next week from camp. We will talk to her then. We didn't want to cut her summer short. And who knows, maybe Corey will be home sooner than later."

"How do you think she will take the news?"

"She will be concerned of course and will want all the details in the form of facts."

"And what about as far as him being gay?"

"I don't think that will sway her one way or the other. She will support him, us."

"She sounds like a levelheaded young lady."

"Oh, she is. Fifteen going on thirty."

Alice nodded. Risa caught something distant in Alice's eyes and couldn't quite put her finger on it. She asked "Do you have children, Alice? I mean, is that okay to ask?"

"Of course! Yes, I have two sons. They are fourteen and sixteen."

Risa looked over to Alice's desk, and noticed for the first time, there were no framed pictures of the family. If Alice noticed this, she did not let on. She continued. "So, you mentioned earlier you spoke with your parents. How are they taking this news?"

"With love. They are the kindest people on this earth. They love Corey unconditionally. Now, Saul's parents... well, that's a whole other can of beans."

"Please, explain."

"Saul and I told Nate and Elaine that Corey had a rare lung disease. I'm not sure they are buying it, but we decided it would be best to not involve them in the truth at this time."

Alice nodded. "Well, you saw how keeping a secret can backfire."

Risa agreed. "Yes, I did. But in this case, Saul seems to feel it would cause too much friction. Having a gay son in Manchester society is bad enough. Having a gay son in Manchester with HIV is pushing it over the edge. And really, it's a shame."

"Yes, it is." She shifted the focus. "Has Saul shared a lot about his childhood? Who his influences were? How family life was for him? You can be brief; I don't want you to feel you have to divulge anything you don't want to."

"To be honest, Alice, since I met him, I've had to piece together parts of his childhood, teen life, and young adult life from the few crumbs he throws me, and of course, any other observations I make on my own. He and his older brother, Steven, were raised by a nanny—a lovely Negro woman named Dolores—who loved, and still loves them, very much. She is currently Nate and Elaine's live-in. She cooks, cleans, and pretty much runs the household. They say she is like family..." Risa looked off through the window. "But I'm here to tell you she will always be relegated to the downstairs living quarters with only one day off a week. She never married, doesn't have kids of her own. You know though, every time Saul and I go to his parents' home, I look forward to seeing Dolores. She is gentle and kind, not a bad bone in her body."

"I take you don't like Nate and Elaine?"

"I do not. I think they are self-absorbed—well, more Elaine than Nate—focusing more on society instead of family."

"Does Steven live nearby?"

"No, he and his wife are physicians in Philadelphia. I've seen them only three times since I married Saul. The first time was at our wedding. I liked them but felt their distance. They couldn't wait to get back on the plane and head home. I saw no love lost between Steven and his parents."

"Was there anyone else in Saul's life who he became close with growing up?"

"Not that I know of."

Alice jotted more notes down. "Okay, let's get back to you, Risa. How are you going to take care of yourself with Corey in the hospital? What are you going to do to maintain your mental health?"

"Oh, believe me, the four-hour ambulance ride back here from New York gave me plenty of time to plan. I am going to be with Corey every day, as much as I can. Together, we are going to beat this thing, so help me Alice. We are going to get him back to normal. And of course, I'll be seeing you. The drive up to Salem will do me good."

Alice asked, "You said something about the apartment in Back Bay?"

"Oh, yes, I plan on using the firm's in-town apartment while Corey is in the hospital. Saul and Rachel and my parents can stay there, too, if need be."

Alice shifted in her chair. "Would you say you are feeling confident that Corey will pull through?"

Risa leaned in. "Alice, I will give him all the love he needs to get through this. Losing him is not an option. I heard what the doctors said about this being a new virus with no cure. But I'm confident they will find something. They must."

"I applaud your tenacity, Risa. It's going to be a long road. Are you prepared for setbacks?"

"Saul and I agree; we will cross those bridges when we come to them."

*** 

After Risa left the office, Alice sat down at her desk and put her head in her hands. A sob escaped from her throat. Without looking, she reached down to her bottom desk drawer where she extracted an eight by ten framed photograph of a little girl with sandy blonde hair and big blue eyes, smiling as if she hadn't a care in the world.

Alice pulled the picture up to her heart and whispered, "Let's give Risa strength, Amy. God help her, she's going to need it."

# Letters to Corey

# CHAPTER NINETEEN

*Massachusetts General Hospital*
*Oncology Unit*
*Monday August 10, 1981*

"Mom! Where did you find Pegleg?"
"In an envelope along with the black marble. In your underwear drawer."
"You went through my underwear drawer?"
"Honey, really. I've been putting your clean clothes away for a while now."
Corey chuckled. "True. Captain Pegleg. How long has it been?"
"You were seven years old."
Corey snuggled into Risa's arm. She had been sitting with him in the hospital bed. He said, "Tell me the story again."
Risa put on her best narration voice. "It was a glorious day in Boston. We took the train—which you just loved, couldn't break you away from the window—and when we arrived at North Station, you said you were hungry. Of course, we had to go to the North End for pizza."
"Oh, God, what I wouldn't do for a slice from Gitano's."
Risa looked at him, "You want me to run and get you some? Maybe for dinner tonight instead of the stuff they call food from here?"
"You'd create quite a scandal. Half the people on this ward get sick at least twelve times a day. Luckily, I've only had to do that twice since I started the medication. Barb says I can probably eat whatever I want when I'm in between doses. Keep telling me the story." He snuggled in closer. Risa tightened her arm around him.
"Okay, so we walked over to Waterfront Park, got a candy apple from a guy selling—"
Corey joined her, they both laughed, "Candy apples!"
"Smarty pants! We crunched on those for a while, then

went over to Faneuil Hall. You were like a kid—"

He joined her again, "In a candy store!"

"Stop it, you stinker!"

"Get to the part where I found Captain Pegleg."

"Okay, okay. So, this older guy with a shock of white hair sticking out of his cap, a scraggly beard and mustache, and huge bushy—"

"Wait, how huge?"

"Huuuuge bushy eyebrows, took one look at you and said, 'Aye ya matey! What's that there on ya shirt? Ya a sailin' man are ye?' And of course, he winked at *me* and stood up a little straighter. You were wearing your favorite blue short sleeved golf shirt with the little white whale patch over the left breast pocket. Your dad got it for you when he went up to Maine."

"Oh, God, yes! I loved that shirt. I think I slept in it until it didn't fit anymore!"

"That you did! And so, the old sailor started to tell us stories of his seafaring days. You were simply enraptured. He regaled us about the long days and nights at sea trying to capture the biggest whale in the history of the world but alas, they never caught it. And then the time when the boat almost sank in the high waves."

Corey put on his best seafaring brogue. "Look out matey's! The waves are comin' at the ship, the wind is blowin' us around, and she might just go under!"

"That's right. And when he was done, he gave you this little wooden figurine and told you it was him, Captain Pegleg! And when you looked at the figurine and then down at his leg, he lifted his pants a little and you could see he had a prosthetic. You almost fainted with joy! He had a real pegleg!"

Corey held the figurine in his hand, turning it this way and that. Risa kissed the top of his head. "You carried that thing around with you twenty-four seven."

"Such a great time with you mom. As always. We really did do a lot, didn't we?"

She hugged him, "And we will *continue* to do so. Let's just get you better."

Corey sat up and stretched his arms. "Can you rub my

neck? It feels so tight." He leaned back as she rubbed his shoulders.

She said, "I brought the black marble, too."

Corey responded, "God that feels good. You brought the Black Pearl?"

"I did. Remember that story?"

"That was great. Mr. Stinky Bones!"

Risa closed her eyes. Her son was losing muscle mass. She rubbed gently, slowly. "The beach at the Maine house. It was August, wasn't it? Yeah it was August, okay, you were twelve, Rachel and your dad were up at the house playing croquet with Grandpa Nate and Dolores."

"Right. We were walking the beach when we smelled something awful."

"You ran to the surf and found that dead fish. You wanted to give it a proper burial. You picked it up and brought it over to me. It was just ghastly!"

Corey chuckled, "It was. But you were a trooper, mom."

"Indeed, I was! We took it up to the seagrass and dug out a little grave. You had collected a bunch of shells and in amongst those was a black marble. You tried to fit it into the dead fish's eye socket and when it wouldn't fit—"

He cut in, "We used it as a grave marker! Your eulogy was right on, mom. You were so good at ad lib. You named him stinky bones!"

She chuckled inwardly. "Yes, we both ended up talking in our best British accent." She moved her hands around his neck and head. "This feel better, honey?"

"Feels so good, mom. Thank you for taking such good care of me." He started to say something else but decided against it. Risa had a feeling it was going to be another apology—there had been many since he became ill—something that she and Saul assured him was not necessary. All that mattered now was that he would get better and stay stress-free.

"I wouldn't have it any other way, son. I love you."

He sighed. "I love you back, Mom."

After a few more minutes, she felt his weight on her chest.

He said without the energy from a few minutes ago, "I'm kind of sleepy all of a sudden. Can I just rest here?"

She held him, "Of course, honey. Take a little snooze. Maybe I will too."

She helped him pull the blanket up around his chin. He said quietly, "Barb will get jealous."

Risa assured him, "Barb will understand."

She listened for his breathing to become steady; cringing at the deep wheeze that was now his new normal. She hated this. She hated every aspect of this horrible virus. But thankfully the experience was softened by Corey's favorite nurse, Barb Van Ness. She was a mensch in the truest form. And Doctor Nori. His calm, gentle bedside manner helped the whole family.

She closed her eyes.

## CHAPTER TWENTY

*The office of Alice Stern*
*Thursday September 3, 1981*

"I feel guilty being here."
"Guilty?" Alice asked.
"I should be with Corey. He had a rough time last night."
"What happened?"
"He had another round of chemotherapy on Tuesday."
"Ah, yes. How was he this morning?"
"Weak. Listless. Couldn't eat. Just sips of water."
"Unfortunately, the drugs have a profound effect on the gastrointestinal tract as well as eradicating the cancer cells."

Risa reached for a tissue. "His hair is thinning out. His gorgeous thick hair is thinning." She shook her head as she covered her face with the tissue. "Goddamn it all." Her body shook with release.

Alice waited.

Risa wiped her eyes and nose then looked at Alice. "The drugs are worse than the virus."

Alice nodded. "They certainly can be."

Risa looked around the room. "I just don't know how to be during these times, Alice. I feel so adrift. Two steps up one step back. Or one step up and three steps back. I feel so…useless."

"How so?"
"Because."
"You can't stop it?"
"Because, Alice, I want to take it all away from him! He's only nineteen. He shouldn't be this sick!"

Alice shifted in her chair. "I certainly understand. A mother never wants to see her child suffer."

Risa took a deep breath. "And those damn interns, or residents, or whatever you call the students. I overheard a conversation the other day that had my blood boiling!"

"What did you hear?"

"Things about my son, his condition. I was talking with Barb at the nurse's station, they had their backs to us. They discussed Corey as if he were, I don't know, some kind of research commodity. One went so far as to say that Corey would not be in this situation today if he had made better choices in his life."

Alice furrowed her brows. "You might want to talk to Doctor Nori about this. Patient information is privileged. And off hand comments are discouraged."

"I think after I returned to Corey's room, Barb might have said something. She's quite protective of Corey."

"Speaking of commodities, a good nurse is a precious one. I'm glad she is there for him."

"Well, I can only imagine what the students say when no one is in earshot." She leaned back onto the couch. "I understand this is a teaching hospital, I understand that they must ask questions, fuss with the chart. But really…"

"Bedside manner should be a course unto itself."

"You'd think."

"So, what's happening at home? How is everything there?"

"Honestly? I've left it up to Saul and Rachel."

"How is Rachel doing with all this?"

"We spoke on Monday at the hospital. She opted to spend the day with Corey instead of going with her friends for a Labor Day sail on the lake. And my parents came for a visit as well. It seemed surrealistic."

"How so?"

"The family together. In a hospital room. With Corey as the main attraction. It was out of place. My mother brought him homemade chicken soup, Rachel and Saul brought pastries from the North End. The party was in the wrong place—it should have been in Manchester with the grill going and dance music playing in the background. That kind of surreal."

Alice nodded as she took notes. "I can see that." She adjusted her glasses and looked back to Risa. "Would you like to share your conversation with Rachel?"

"She said that she has one friend she confides in. And this friend is very loyal to Rachel, knows how to keep a confidence."

"Another precious commodity. Teenagers are notorious for saying one thing and doing another."

"This friend is wise beyond her years as well. I'm glad Rachel has her. She needs someone her age." Risa clasped her hands together in her lap. "And I've not been very present for her. It's hard on me but I cannot put anything in front of Corey. Saul and my mother have been instrumental in keeping pace with Rachel. She's now in the tenth grade, at high school." Risa withdrew a tissue from the box. "She doesn't want him to die."

Alice nodded. "A very real fear."

"I told her the same, and that we were going to do everything in our power to not let that happen."

"Were they close growing up?"

"Yes, until Corey reached the teenage years, but when they needed to be, they were a team."

"Sounds normal." She shifted in her chair and crossed her legs. "So, you. Let's talk a little about you. You're right there on the front lines every day. How is this fairing? Are you sleeping? Eating?"

Risa looked down at her nails then folded her fingers in toward her palms. "I've been letting a few things go. Am I sleeping? Restless at best. Eating? I eat when he eats. When he is sick, it's hard."

"Sounds like you want to share his suffering."

"I do. If I take half of it, it won't be so overwhelming for him. If I can just bear some of the weight." Risa absently looked off toward the bookcase. "It's not fair Alice. None of this is fair."

"When it comes to fairness, and the ways of the universe, aren't we *all* warriors on this road to humanity?"

Risa looked at her. "Yes, I suppose we are, aren't we?"

Alice asked, "Now, you've said you had two sisters. Are you close?"

"They both live on the west coast. We've spoken by phone and they know what is going on. Both have offered to come home to see us. I promised them a visit when Corey is up and running again. I don't want too much activity around him."

"Do your sisters have children?"

"Franny has three, all grown. She's six years older than me. Helen is three years older."

"Are they being supportive?"

"Luckily, they are."

"Why would you say, luckily?"

Risa thought about it for a moment then said, "We were raised to accept all walks of life."

Alice frowned, "But yet you said if word leaked out about Corey—"

Risa cut her off, "Not from my side of the family. I just happened to marry into a walk of life that does not recognize so-called abnormal behavior."

Alice nodded. "Well, there is that, isn't there?"

Risa explained, "I don't understand the behavior, but he's my son, and he's sick, and that is *all* that matters right now." She used the crumpled tissue in her hand to dab at her eyes. "And the gossip of what he is sick with would spread like wildfire and neither Saul nor I can handle that right now."

"This is tough stuff, Risa. I'm glad you're here to get it out."

She said, around the tears, "I don't think I could handle it any other way. I keep having this dream that I am driving a runaway train and when I reach for the break lever, it snaps off in my hands."

Alice said gently, "When we go through something as traumatic as this, there are bound to be nightmares." She waited for Risa to compose herself. "Tell me, how is Corey taking all of this?"

"He is frightened. Tries to keep a stiff upper lip, but I know."

"It's not uncommon. The hospital, the tests, the results, the underlying issues. It's enough to make anyone unsettled. He is quite vulnerable right now."

"He is." Risa sighed then shook her head slightly, "Sometimes I get so angry."

"Angry. At?"

"At Corey for getting himself into this mess. But I swallow it down. He doesn't need to see or hear that in my voice. Things must stay calm."

Alice put her pad and pen down on the table, picked up her glass of water and took a sip, then regarded Risa. She said, "Anger is a beast. There are many components of it, just like the many components of keeping a secret or telling a white lie. Right now, though, I want to ask a difficult question. Can we do that?"

Risa sat up straighter. "I guess it depends upon nature of the question."

Alice leaned forward. "Are you angry at the disease or," she hesitated for a moment then said, "more to the point, the fact that Corey's lifestyle and subsequent circumstances are wreaking havoc in your life?"

Risa let out a harumph. "Nothing like getting to the point."

"Well, what's the point of being here if we can't *get* to the point?"

Risa nodded tightly, her lips pursed, and said nothing.

Alice said, "I'm not asking this to *add* to your anger. I just want us to visualize *why* you are angry."

Risa clenched her jaw. "I don't know." She raised her voice, her arms going up from her sides. "Everything. *Everything!* Things were going along so smoothly. My life, *his* life, almost perfect! And then *whammo!*"

Alice nodded then said matter-of-factly, "Whammo. Your son is gay then contracts a deadly virus."

Risa looked down at her feet. The polish on her toes was starting to chip. She thought she should really start wearing close-toed shoes. She turned and looked at the clock behind her. A few more minutes. She swallowed her anger at Alice for putting into words what she had long buried. She turned to face her then whispered hoarsely, "I can't do this right now."

Alice nodded. "You *are* safe here, Risa. There is no time limit for the truth."

THERAPY NOTE:
*Anger stage, denial of incurable disease, convinced he will win this battle, her life is centered on his, control of environment very important right now, she teeters between two realities. Relationship with Rachel sketchy, pursue. AS*

# Letters to Corey

# CHAPTER TWENTY-ONE

*MGH Oncology Unit*
*Tuesday September 8, 1981*

Risa was feeling more positive than she had since Corey's infusion from last week. He had requested a turkey sandwich from Cardullo's on Beacon Street, just around the corner from the apartment, and Risa gladly ordered enough food for the family, not allowing the recent discovery of more lesions on his legs and abdomen deter her from keeping her spirits up.

"He's hungry!" She excitedly told Saul that morning. "And I'm Jewish! What better a combination?" She had laughed for the first time in what seemed like weeks.

Saul was upbeat too, "Oh, this is great news, honey."

"Peg is coming by while I go out. She's been such a godsend. Her *and* Walt." Peg had stepped in unconditionally for the family as an all-around surrogate. If Saul had a long court case, Peg would drive to Manchester to ferry Rachel to her various after-school activities or to bring her to Boston. She replenished Risa's suitcases, brought extra clothes for Corey. And Walt, the kids' pediatrician, took a vested interest in this new virus and had many long conversations with Doctor Nori regarding Corey's treatment plan. Risa felt solidarity; with everyone rallying around Corey he was bound to beat this thing!

When Risa came back after picking up food, Peg was already with Corey, and they were cackling about something. Corey's laughter was music to her ears. Her heart soared. "What did I miss?"

"Good grief, Reese, what, did you buy out the store?"

Risa set the bags of food on one of the chairs. "Just some much needed good sustenance for *all* of us!" She said to Peg, "I got you a pastrami on rye."

"Oh, that was sweet of you."

Risa withdrew another wax-paper wrapped sandwich and handed it to Corey, "Are you ready to eat?"

Corey reached for it, "I'm starving!" He closed his eyes as he bit into the thick gourmet sandwich. "Oh, my God." He mumbled around the food in his mouth. "This is amazing."

Risa smiled. "So good to see your appetite bounce back."

Peg unwrapped her sandwich, "Corey, you want to tell your mom our plan?"

Corey nodded and swallowed. It took a moment for him to get it all down. He took a sip of water. "Maybe you should tell her."

"Oh? Tell me what?"

"He wants to me to shave his head."

Risa's half-smile turned into a frown. "He wants you to do *what*?"

Corey sat forward, "Mom, I'm losing it daily and it really looks like hell. Shaved heads are cool now, the 'in' thing!! I can wear a turban, a hat, a cabbie hat, all the cool things that—"

Risa looked at Peg and sighed. "Oh, brother."

Peg said quickly, "We thought you might feel that way, but listen, it *will* grow back, and even *thicker,* I'm told."

Risa stepped over to her son, running her fingers gently through his hair. It was true, he was losing it daily. There were a few patches in the back where she could see the skin of his skull. He looked up at her with such pleading eyes that she had to choke back a sob.

Corey picked up where Peg left off. "Remember all those wigs I used to try on at the theatre?"

Risa chided. "Don't even think about it."

The three of them looked at one another in silence, then Risa shook her head and relented. "I knew there would be trouble leaving the two of you alone. Let's wait until I can tell your father, so he won't have a heart attack when he sees you."

*\*\*\**

Later, after Peg had gone home and Corey settled in for his afternoon nap, Risa met Saul at Corey's door and whispered, "He just dozed off. Let's go down to the solarium."

Saul folded his jacket over his arm and closed the door quietly behind them. They walked, hand in hand, down the hall. Once seated, Saul said, "I spoke with a colleague today, someone I met at a conference last year in New York. Turns out Corey is not the only discrimination case at NYU. Seems several students, and not just freshmen, are on the firing line. Some are not as sick as Corey, others are worse."

"Did you talk to him about the possibility of a lawsuit?"

He harumphed. "Taking on New York University will probably never occur. Ken said HIV is too new. Lawyers are running away from cases because no precedence has been established."

Risa shook her head. "Wow. Just, wow."

Saul said, "This is going to be an ugly war, Risa."

They remained quiet for a moment then Risa asked, "So, how are you faring with all of this? We rarely get a chance to talk these days."

"I'm handling it the best way I know how. Work helps. I'm busy with Rachel and the house, with keeping my parents at bay, with keeping Corey's spirits up."

"But how are you dealing with your own feelings around it?"

Saul remained quiet, his eyes darkening in the dimming daylight of the solarium. "I don't know. I have tough moments. Of course, I love him unconditionally." He thought for a moment then added, "It doesn't mean I'm completely comfortable with his choices."

"It's not a choice, Saul."

"I know. I'm speaking about his choices in being too carefree with his intimate life."

Risa nodded. "Yes. I struggle with that too." She sighed deeply. "Saul, I wonder if things would have been different if he had come to us before college, if I had been more forthright, if I had stepped up to the plate and shared what I knew with you so we could intercept things together, as a team.."

"Reese. I agree. You should have come to me. But you didn't cause this. It's not your fault." He pulled her hand to his lips and kissed the back of it, turning toward her. "I miss you. Us."

"I do, too." She closed her eyes and kept his hand near her cheek. It felt so warm and simple, she had missed him too. "Maybe as soon as Corey gets back on his feet, we can reassess our next move. Let's think about doing something as a family. Perhaps get out of town to a quiet island somewhere."

"Now that *would* be nice."

They sat with their own thoughts. Their conversation had been so innocent, loving. They were a team.

But Risa's world was unbalanced. It revolved solely around Corey's well-being. Everything else fell by the wayside: her co-chairs at CAP were understanding under the circumstances and assured her the seat was still hers, the stage and roles would still be there, and her friends knew Corey was sick, but not with what. Her exercise routines, tennis games, date nights with her husband, quick weekend getaways to Hilton Head, and the carefree life; all on backburners.

Saul interrupted her thoughts. "Hungry?"

"I had my sandwich earlier. I got one for you, corned beef on rye with Dijon and pickle. It's in the fridge. I'll get it for you, we can head down to the cafeteria. I could use a cup of java."

"Sounds perfect, honey."

"Let's just peek in on Corey before we go."

He was still asleep. Risa tiptoed in, dropped Saul's coat on a chair then kissed him gently on the forehead. He looked so peaceful. Even his breathing seemed easier, steadier. Maybe the drugs were starting to work. She held on to that glimmer of hope as she joined her husband in the hallway.

"Oh, by the way, Corey wants Peg to shave his head."

"Is that right?" He chuckled.

The elevator door shushed open, and they walked in. "They seem to think it will look very hip, cool."

Saul thought about it for a moment, crossed his hands in front of him as the car slowly dropped to the mezzanine level. When they exited, he smiled and said, "It just might, at that."

# CHAPTER TWENTY-TWO

*Friday September 18, 1981*

"Mom," Corey said, "take a few days to yourself. You've been here non-stop since I was admitted. You need to take care of things."

Risa narrowed her eyebrows, "Like?"

"Well, first, your nails look like hell, your hair is crazy thick and needs attention. And you're still wearing summer clothes. Your make-up is kind of uneven. Are you sleeping in those clothes?"

Risa folded her arms in front of her chest and took on the offended mother role. "Well, how do you like that? My own son telling me I'm looking haggard!"

He laughed and reached for her hand, "Oh, Mom, just take the weekend, okay? I'll be fine. Barb is on duty; Rachel is coming by tomorrow with Peg and we are going to shave off what's left of my hair."

She instinctively reached out and ran her fingers through his bangs, a sigh caught in the middle of her chest. "So, the big day is tomorrow?"

"Yes, and just think. When you come back on Monday, we'll *both* have different hairstyles." He laughed and cleared his throat, "Well, you will."

Risa sat down next to him on the bed. "Okay, you're the boss. If you think you'll be okay."

"Mom, I feel darned good. So, seize the day!"

She kissed him on his forehead. "Okay. What can I do before I leave?"

He smirked. "Shut the door?"

She shook her head. "Yep, the drugs are working. You're back to your old snarky self."

"And don't you forget it, sister."

"Sister?" She shook her head as she gathered her belongings.

\*\*\*

Corey gave his mother half an hour to make sure she was gone before picking up the phone. He placed a person-to-person call.

"Can you be here by dinner time?"

"If I have to rent a private plane, I'll be there."

"God, I miss you."

"I miss you, too."

\*\*\*

Later that afternoon, when Risa arrived home after her appointments and shopping, she was startled to see Elaine's car parked in the driveway. Risa pulled in next to her, turned off the engine and stepped out of the car. "Elaine?"

Her mother-in-law got out of the car, slammed the door, and strode toward her. "Is Saul home yet?"

Risa immediately tensed. "Not yet. As you can see, I just got home. He's on the five-thirty train. What's the matter?"

She put her hands on her hips. "When were the two of you going to tell us?" She looked at Risa's head. "And what the hell did you do to your hair?"

Risa guarded herself, Elaine's delivery setting her on high alert. "I had it cut and styled. But what are you talking about, Elaine? Tell you what?"

"When were you going to tell us, that Corey is *queer?*"

Risa almost dropped her belongings. "*What?*"

"Oh, please, don't expect me to believe you *don't know!*"

Risa said, "Why don't we talk in the house?"

"Is Rachel home?" Elaine demanded.

"No. She's staying with—"

"Good," she said curtly, cutting Risa off. "She shouldn't have to hear this."

Once inside, Elaine turned around. "You'd better start from the beginning, Risa. I cannot tell you my patience is running out!"

"Please, will you just calm down? Sit down, take off your coat. Do you want a glass of wine? Scotch?"

Elaine removed her coat, tossing it over a dinette chair. "Let's dispense with the niceties, I want answers!"

"Sit down, Elaine. We can talk but not when you're like this. What happened?"

Instead of sitting down, she paced while Risa slipped out of her coat and dropped it much like Elaine did, over a chair. Elaine said, as her heels clacked on the wood floor. "I had a meeting in town today and thought, gee wouldn't it be nice to see my grandson? So, I went to the hospital. When I arrived up to his room, he was kissing another *man*! A *shvartze*!"

This caught Risa off guard. It wasn't that Corey was kissing another man, it was more about who it might have been. "Did you talk to him? Them?"

"No! I didn't talk to...*him, them*! I was too shocked! I left the hospital immediately!"

Risa reached into the refrigerator, pulled out a bottle of wine and poured herself a hefty amount. "Elaine, Saul and I decided to keep Corey's proclivity quiet. We felt—"

She cut her off. "Does he have this gay plague or whatever the hell it's called?"

"It's called HIV, Elaine."

Elaine kept her eyes on Risa. "Uh huh. I had a feeling he wasn't quite right. How *does* Saul feel about all this?"

A voice came from behind them at the door. "How does Saul feel about what?"

Risa and Elaine turned to look in his direction. Risa tried to signal him with her eyes, but he was looking at her head.

"Your hair, wow!"

Her hand went immediately to her bangs. "Do you like it?"

He cocked his head and smiled. "Well, it's very striking. I like it." He turned his attention to his mother. "Mom, nice to see you! To what do we owe this unexpected visit?" He took off his overcoat, walked down the hall to the closet, hung it up, came back and called over his shoulder as he went to the liquor cart in the den. "Anybody want some scotch?"

Neither answered.

He came back in, swirling the thick tawny-colored liquid. "Why all the stern faces?"

Risa said, "I think we all need to sit down."

Saul stopped short. "What now?"

They walked into the living room. Saul grabbed Risa's hand and pulled her back some. He mouthed, "What?"

Risa shook her head.

Elaine sat down in the wingback chair while Risa and Saul opposite her on the couch.

"Well?" Saul asked.

Elaine spoke up. "When were you and your wife going to tell us that your son is a faggot?"

Saul took a sharp intake of breath. "What? How did —"

She cut him off. "I thought I would visit my grandson today. When I arrived, he was kissing a man. A *shvartze* no less!"

Saul's eyes went blank for a moment, then he looked at Risa and murmured, "A... who could this be?"

Risa shook her head. "I have no idea."

Elaine's voice rose again. "And he's got this gay plague, this *HIV* plague! *When* were you planning on telling us?"

Saul cleared his throat. "Mom, we decided to keep it quiet for Corey's sake."

"But how and *why* could you keep it from *us*?"

Saul took a long swallow of his scotch. "Look mom, maybe it wasn't right to keep this from you, but we have our reasons."

"Do you condone it?" She looked at them one at a time.

Saul answered, "Mom, it's complicated."

"Yes, it's always complicated, isn't it, Saul."

He flinched. "What are you implying, mother?"

Elaine looked nonchalantly at Risa, "Risa, did Saul ever tell you about—"

Saul leaned in sharply, his voice low and threatening. "Not *now,* mother!"

Risa looked from Elaine back to Saul. "What? Tell me what?"

Elaine sat back, triumphant. "I guess not."

Saul stood abruptly. "So, now you know about Corey. Why not just leave it status quo?"

"Don't you think it's about time you let the cat out of the bag?"

"Look, all I want to do is change my clothes, have a cocktail, then have a nice relaxing dinner with my wife. I don't have to tell you we've been under quite a strain of late! We don't need this extra added turmoil! Don't you think we've had enough already?"

Risa took his hand in hers. "We don't have to talk about *this* or *anything* right now for that matter." Then she turned to face Elaine. "Why don't we call you and Nate later?"

Elaine shook her head. "Oh, for heaven's sake stop babying him. I can't believe that after twenty-five years of marriage you don't know about Saul's past!"

Saul clanked his glass onto the table, the liquid sloshing out. He stood, and in two strides was in his mother's face. "How dare you come into our house—"

She cocked an eyebrow. "We bought the house for you, remember?"

For a moment, Risa thought Saul might strike her. The tension in the room was palpable.

Risa stood. "I think it's time for you to leave, Elaine."

Elaine also rose but did not make for the kitchen and her coat. "You two might want to have a conversation. Maybe Risa, you will understand your husband a bit better." She turned on her heel and mumbled. "My grandson is a faggot with a shvartze. This is going to kill Nathan."

Risa emphasized, "Enough! Please leave!"

They waited until Elaine backed out of the driveway. The silence in the house was jarring. Saul went to the fireplace, leaned on the mantel piece, and sipped his scotch.

Risa sat back down on the couch. "Saul, I swear on my life Corey has not mentioned a man in his life."

"Just one more thing to add to an already full plate."

Risa gently pried. "Honey, what do we need to talk about? What was Elaine referring to?"

"I owe you an explanation."

"Yes, you do."

Saul ran his finger along the faces in a framed photograph

of the family taken four summers ago at Tanglewood Music Center. He murmured, "Such a beautiful weekend, don't you think?"

Risa nodded, "It was magical."

"Yes. It was a time when all of us were in complete synch with each other."

"I will never forget that weekend, Saul."

"And now, years later we come upon this unexpected fork in the road,"

They were silent. Appliances ticked; the furnace rumbled.

Saul turned to look at her, his eyes tired, his body losing some of its stature bravado. "I had an experience when I was young, Risa. When I was just a boy."

She waited, a small relief flooding over her. "Go on."

He looked down at his shoes. "I have an uncle that we don't talk about. His name is George. My father's brother. He lives somewhere in California now, but he used to live here, with us, when Steven and I were young." Saul paced in front of the fireplace. "When I was eight, George came to live with us. Steven and I didn't know exactly why he was there, but as kids we understood that adults did things that children had no business knowing about. So, Uncle George was just…there. We liked it because he didn't go to work like our dad had to do, and you know the story behind our mother—never there, even when she was."

He finished the rest of his scotch, set the glass down on a small table then sat down in the wingback chair to face his wife. "Uncle George was different from my father. He liked to instigate a dare or two, always willing to play with us. He would tell us these great stories about his travels, which we believed because that's what rapt kids do—believe in adults. He was most entertaining." He looked off and smiled, a memory passing in front of his eyes. "And we were drawn to him. He let us be kids, felt we should be allowed to be little boys, without so many rules and regulations. And then, one day George decided he liked me more than he liked Steven. It was mid-summer, hot. He promised me we would hike to a spot nestled between pine trees, where it was cooler. Steven had a swimming lesson that day at the country club. Well, once we got to the spot in the pines, he began touching me. First, it was just a hug, an arm around my shoulders. Then as the day went on, he pulled me up onto his lap." Saul's face went dark, his mouth drawn in. He looked down at his shoes again and then at his wife. His voice was low. "It went on until Fall; he would corner me in the house when no one else was around, or when Dolores was busy in the kitchen. It went on for almost a year. I had just turned ten, Steven was fourteen."

This struck Risa to her core.

"Then Steven found us in the wine cellar one evening."

Risa asked quietly, "Did he tell your parents?"

"Oh, yes. He most certainly did." Saul sighed and looked off, "And George was gone the next day. My parents—mostly my mother—believed it was my fault. That I egged George on."

Risa was aghast. "Egged…*what*…egged him *on*? A *ten-year-old*?"

"It gets worse. You see, Risa, I knew what happened between us was wrong. But he was the only adult, aside from Dolores, who showed me any friendship at all. Any love. He was my best friend."

Risa shook her head. "It was *rape*!"

The word hung in the air.

Saul closed his eyes.

When he opened them, he looked directly at his wife. "Did he violate me? Not exactly, so it wasn't rape, per se. It was oral and touching, kissing. But, you see, I liked it, Reese. Letting him touch me meant it was something only he and I shared. A secret language only he and I knew how to translate. I felt emboldened by it, as much as a ten-year-old could feel. I was special, Reese. And then they sent him away. It was like someone ripped my arm out of the socket. And then, a little later I learned that Steven told my parents it was my fault—which is another reason Steven, and I are estranged. I never forgave him for that."

Risa stood and walked to her husband. "Saul. That was manipulation in the worst way!" She took his head to her chest and held it there—much as she had done with Corey that first night in the hospital. "You were *not* responsible for that transgression!"

Saul's body shook. "Oh, God, Reese. And now…now, Corey…our son. Our *son*!" His tears ran hard, raw, broken. He leaned into her, and she held him as his body crumpled into hers.

## CHAPTER TWENTY-THREE

*MGH Oncology Unit*
*Sunday September 20, 1981*

When Risa entered Corey's room, she found him dozing. She studied him quietly while putting her belongings on an empty chair near the bed. A deep pang of sorrow ricocheted in her chest. He had a boyfriend and kept it from them.

A powder blue knitted cap sat askew on his head. She almost reached over to set it right but decided not to wake him. He needed his rest. As she left the room, she thought perhaps the man he was with had given it to him.

She approached the nursing station. Barb looked up from her paperwork. "Mrs. Shapiro! I didn't even recognize you at first! Your hair is stunning! Well, you're stunning no matter what."

"Thank you, Barb. Corey convinced me it was time. It's been an adjustment, but what hasn't been these days?"

She smiled. "He's doing well today. Ate a full breakfast, even finished the god awful shake I made for him! We took a walk down to the solarium and back a few times."

"How is his back? He says he gets so stiff."

"Doctor Nori approved physical therapy for him. Someone from the department will be up in a while to get an assessment. They will work with him right in his room, in the bed most likely."

"I'm pleased to hear that."

The elevator doors opened and a group of white-coated men and women emerged. Barb murmured. "Here they come, the not so grand-round players."

Risa nodded, "Thus it begins. I hope they leave him alone this morning. I really don't want him disturbed."

Barb stood up and approached the attending physician. While she was doing that, Risa noticed a young black man heading down the hall toward Corey's room.

She followed him, her flat slipper-like shoes squeaking quietly on the linoleum floor. When he stopped to knock on the door with his knuckles, Risa caught up with him.

"Excuse me."

He turned around to face her. Their eyes locked.

She asked, "Are you by chance Corey's friend?"

His voice was guarded, "Uhm. Yes, I am."

She looked him over briefly then extended her hand. "I'm Corey's mom."

He responded to her gesture, his posture relaxing. "You are even more beautiful in person. I've seen pictures."

"Thank you. And you are?"

"Michael, Michael Whitman." He was still holding her hand. "From New York."

Risa was immediately taken with his deep, sotto voice. His firm handshake exuded warmth and softness. She said quietly, "He's resting now, and I don't want him disturbed. Would you like to go to the cafeteria for a cup of coffee?"

He smiled, "Yes, I would."

Risa and Michael walked back down the hall to the elevators in silence. She was aware of his presence: tall, well-dressed, handsome, with a smile that shined from the darkness of his skin.

Once settled in with their beverages, Michael offered, "I'm sure this is all a bit of a shock for you. Me being here. Corey told me he had not shared our relationship with you and your husband."

Risa answered, "Well, to be honest, yes, but these days, one cannot discount the possibilities of shocks." She thought about the last two days with Saul: finally learning of his childhood experiences. "But, since you and I are here, let's get to know one another a bit, shall we?"

"I would like that, Mrs. Shapiro."

"Please, call me Risa."

"Alright then, Risa." He took a sip of his coffee. "Where shall we start?"

"You. Tell me about Michael."

"Okay, sure. Well, I was born and raised in Philadelphia,

went to the Harvard School of Design, ended up in New York with a small architectural firm six years ago and that's where I've been ever since."

"Where did you meet Corey?"

"Through friends. Last year."

She immediately understood why Corey didn't want to come home over the summer break. This was obviously the 'friend' he was staying with in New York. "Do you mind if I ask how old you are?"

"Of course not, I'm twenty-nine."

"Curious. Why would you have a relationship with someone so much younger than you?"

"I don't look at age, necessarily. He was great to talk to, we had a lot of laughs right off the bat. And" he hesitated, "I don't have to tell you how incredibly handsome he is."

Risa nodded even though Corey's body mass was shrinking, his hair was gone, his eyes were sinking deeper into his face, not to mention the new lesions. "He is."

"My friends asked me the same questions, Mrs. uhm, Risa. And my answer is always the same. Sometimes you can't figure out why you choose someone to be intimate with. It just happens. He stole my heart."

Risa blushed, had a moment of unchecked jealousy, then agreed. "Yes, he is a thief of hearts indeed." She sipped her coffee. "But how about now, now with his current medical condition?"

Michaels eyes darkened. "I have no problem with his HIV status. He seems to think he's going to beat this. So, I'm on board with him, whatever he thinks is going to happen."

"But you have your doubts?"

He looked away from her.

She waited.

When he turned his gaze back, he said quietly, "This is a very scary virus. I've lost several friends to it. Some days you think you're out of the woods, and then…"

Risa did not want him to finish his sentence. She ventured a step. "How do you think he got this, Michael?"

He anticipated. "I've been tested, and I am negative. When

Corey started feeling ill, I recognized the signs. After a few weeks of him not getting any better I took him to the campus health center, which is where they transferred him to Sloan. You know the rest, of course."

Risa sat back in her chair, the coffee threatening to rise in her throat. "Thank you." She didn't know what else to say.

"Mrs. Shapiro," Michael began, "This must be so overwhelming for you. There are so many questions left unanswered. Believe me, my family is terrified too."

Risa asked, "Does your family know about you? About you and Corey?"

"They do. But they are worried about me—a black gay man in a very white world. They've met Corey, though. They love him."

Again, Risa felt the sting of reality. *His* parents knew about Corey, they *loved* him! She and Saul were still unearthing secret after secret. Omissions and lies—what was worse?

Risa had a lot to discuss with Alice. She looked off toward a table full of white-coated men and women. "The doctors..." she intoned quietly. "They haven't got a clue, do they?" Words stuck in her throat. She felt her eyes fill. Everything was too much at that moment.

Michael reached out with his hand and set it gently on top of hers. "Unfortunately, Mrs. Shapiro, this virus spreads so fast that none of us have a clue. It's turning the gay population on its head."

Risa leaned forward sharply. "Corey is going to beat this. We all must have faith and confidence."

Michael tried to smile, tightening his hand on hers. "I hope he does. Make it through this. I will never show him doubt." He added matter-of-factly, "I care for Corey. And while I know he's in good hands here, and surrounded by his family, I won't abandon him. You see, Mrs. Shapiro, Risa, I..."

She took a deep breath then let it out. "You love him, don't you?"

He fixed his eyes on hers. "Yes, I do. I truly love him."

\*\*\*

Corey was awake when Risa and Michael entered his room. At first, Corey was startled, seeing his mother with his lover. But then calmed when Risa said, "Look who I just had coffee with!"

Corey eyed Michael. Michael approached Corey and kissed him on the forehead. "Your mother is one heck of a lady, Corey."

Corey held his hand then finally looked at his mother, who was still standing in the doorway. "Holy cow, look at you! Your hair is—turn around!"

Risa stepped into the room and pirouetted. "You like?"

"You look fabulous! And the clothes! I love the look, mom! So very Reba McIntyre! Nails and toes?"

Risa nodded, "As prescribed."

Michael sat down on the bed and cupped Corey's face in his hand. "How are you feeling today, babe?"

"Better now." He looked over at his mother. "Come on, Mom, plenty of room for the three of us."

She sat at the end of the bed.

Corey said, "So I assume you talked to Grandma Elaine."

"We did, and it's all fine, son. Do *not* worry about a thing."

"So, she knows everything?"

"Yes, pretty much."

"I'm sorry, mom. I never thought for a minute she'd show up unannounced." He reached for her hand.

She took it. "It's all under control honey. You just concentrate on getting better, that's all that counts. And now, I'm going to make a few phone calls from downstairs, give you some privacy."

Michael stood. "I hope I'm not in the way here. I'm headed back to New York tomorrow morning."

Risa took his hands in hers. "Not for a moment." Then she said to Corey, "Dad is going to pick Rachel up at North Station. We can order from the deli across the street. Michael, just write down what you would like, too."

He nodded and thanked her.

When his mother left the room, Corey pulled Michael to him. "Well, that went well! She likes you."

Michael kissed Corey on his cheeks. "And how would you know that?"

"She wouldn't have offered food." He laughed, then coughed. Deep and phlegmy.

Michael reached for the emesis basin and tissues.

\*\*\*

Risa went downstairs to the little chapel off from the main lobby. It was empty, eerily quiet. She sat down in one of the pews and gazed at the intricate stained-glass window over the dais. Her heart felt swollen, her body laden. A darkness settled around her soul.

Corey had a boyfriend; another part of his life where she was not included.

She felt overwhelmed, small.

Insignificant.

And afraid.

Afraid she was going to lose her place.

## CHAPTER TWENTY-FOUR

*The Office of Alice Stern*
*Thursday September 24, 1981*

Alice was writing as fast as she could. She said, "You must be relieved regarding Saul's truth. You felt you knew, anyhow."

"I am. It *had* to have been something like that. And frankly, it all makes perfect sense."

"How do you feel about all this?" She looked up.

"Glad he finally got it out of his system. Not happy about how it came to pass, but then I remembered what you said about secrets revealing themselves when the time is right, despite the circumstances. And believe me, I was ready to deck Elaine a good one for her nasty attitude. She was just awful!"

Alice nodded. "I'm sure she was. And how do you feel about all these secrets?"

"Scattered. Adrift. Angry. Sad. What else is there?"

"I get the sense that there is some discomfort with how close Michael and Corey seem to be."

Risa nodded, "It was yet another thing he kept from us. And yes, I felt a little out of place with them. Like I didn't belong."

"Like the mother?" Alice asked.

"I don't understand."

"When we see our kids outgrow us—if you will—and find someone in their life their own age, it typically puts us second in line. It's natural, of course. But in your situation, I imagine there are many tender boundaries. And Michael is really the first one to test those waters."

"And there is absolutely nothing wrong with him. Saul and Rachel like him. Barb, the nurse, likes him. I like him. But I can't help but feel…I don't know."

"Jealous?"

Risa blushed. "Yes. Very."

Alice smiled, "Understandable."

Risa became serious. "What really rankles me, though, Alice, is how Michaels family knows about Corey. And here Saul and I are floundering around in the dark from day to day. I must wonder what else Corey is keeping from us."

"Can you talk to him about it?"

"I plan on it, tonight. We're going to be alone. I promised him a pizza."

"Sounds like his appetite is doing well. I'm glad to hear that. So, tell me, what do you hope to accomplish with the conversation?"

"I want to ask him why. Why did he keep all this from us. What made him feel he had to. Was it something I did? Saul did? I just want to know how he sees us."

Alice agreed. "I think these are very valid points to bring up. Perhaps he will be ready to answer the questions."

"Sometimes I feel like I never really knew him." Risa looked down at her slacks, pulling an unseen thread from a seam. "Was I that blind that I just saw the boy I wanted him to be? And when he turned out to be something different, did that drive him further away?"

Alice nodded while writing. "This is good. Keep going. You are on the right track."

"I don't know. I'm not sure I can admit to such a grand failure."

Alice looked at her, her glasses slipping down to the end of her nose. "A grand failure?"

Risa looked around the room. "I don't know."

Alice pushed her glasses up, "Please, try to dig a little deeper."

"I don't think I can right now. The thing is, Alice. All this therapy is like a double-edged sword."

"What do you mean?"

"I like coming here and unloading. It's safe and I think it's helping me in a big way. But to dig deeper, it feels too chancy."

"Chancy, how?"

"Like I'm just going to, I don't know. It's easier to put the day-to-day grind in its place right now. Can you help me do that instead of dig deeper?"

Alice nodded, shrugged slightly. "We can certainly do that. But there will come a time when you might need to get all this out."

"I realize that. But not now. I must stay strong. When Corey starts to heal, I can let go."

Alice set her pad down. "I must commend you on your tenacity, Risa. You have a tremendous reserve. We are making good progress here, and part of that progress is digging deep. But like I said in the beginning, this is your hour, however you choose to spend it. I'm here to guide you, not trip you up."

Risa looked at her watch. The session was over. "Thank you. I'll call for the next appointment, would that be okay?"

"Of course, it is."

She stood. "Thank you, Alice. You're a godsend."

When Risa left the office, Alice closed the door, sat down at her desk, and pulled the picture of Amy from the bottom drawer of her desk, setting it in front of her.

"There we go." She kissed the tips of her fingers and laid them gently on the glass of the photo on her daughter's cheek. "It may be some time before I hear from Risa again. Some of them come back, some just disappear into the ethers of their denial. We find comfort in denial. I know this only too well. It took me a lot of therapy to free myself from the guilt after you died. I couldn't have stopped that car if I wanted to. It was to be your fate, our fate. I miss you so…my sunshine."

THERAPY NOTE:
*Stages of grief now mixed with stages of denial. Question devotion to her son, obsession? See notes. AS*

# Letters to Corey

## CHAPTER TWENTY-FIVE

*MGH Oncology Unit*
*Friday September 25, 1981*

Pizza night did not happen.

Risa positioned Corey into the crook of her arm on the hospital bed. The less aggressive drug therapy was anything but. His reaction was violent, his system revolting against the poison coursing through his bloodstream. After spending most of the night vomiting until he passed out, he was now sleeping soundly with an oxygen mask on his face, two IV lines; one in each arm.

Risa was ragged. Saul had been with them most of the night and managed to get a few hours of sleep at the apartment before going to work. Risa closed her eyes. Restless images of the last day and a half raced elliptically from one eye to the other. She needed a shower and a change of clothes and would not leave him for any length of time until Peg arrived at six.

The door opened quietly.

Risa opened her eyes.

Barb padded ghostlike to the bed, whispering, "Good, he's finally resting." She checked his IV lines, the oxygen supply. "When you get a moment, come on down to the nursing station."

Risa made the 'okay' sign with her fingers.

She sat for another ten or fifteen minutes then slowly extricated her arm from underneath his shoulders. He shuffled a bit but did not wake up. She adjusted his oxygen mask, knitted cap, and blankets, then stealthily slipped out of bed, smoothing down her wrinkled, stained clothes.

At the nursing station, Barb grabbed a sheaf of papers then had Risa follow her to a small conference room near the solarium.

Once seated, Barb tried to sound professional, but her voice gave her away. "Risa, Corey's lab values came back this morning. We took them two days ago. When he was feeling good. It's not what we were hoping for."

Risa felt her throat go dry.

"Doctor Nori wants to talk with you and your husband. Any chance Saul can be here around three o'clock?"

"I'll call him. He'll be here."

"Good, okay. I'll get with Nori now." Barb put her hand on Risa's arm.

Risa looked away.

Barb had no words.

\*\*\*

When Corey woke, it was almost two o'clock in the afternoon. A lab tech came by to draw blood, but he couldn't find a good vein.

Risa tried to keep the annoyance of her voice. "Perhaps you should wait a while? He's already so weak."

Corey's voice was a whisper. He moved the oxygen mask from his mouth down to his chin. "Yeah, I can't afford to lose anything else for a day or two."

The tech stowed his gear. "No problem, we can get it later. Take it easy, Corey."

Corey licked his dry lips. "How about a few ice chips? Maybe later I can try some soup. I can't decide if I'm hungry or nauseous. My stomach muscles are killing me."

Risa stroked his face. It was so smooth, no longer growing hair. "I know honey. I'll be right back with the ice chips. Anything else? Maybe a Coke?"

"Yeah, maybe that will help. I feel so weak. Maybe I need a sugar rush."

"Sit tight. Your dad and I are going to meet with Doctor Nori in a bit. Peg said she'd come a little earlier. Do you want anything from the outside world?"

"Maybe a joint?"

Risa stopped in her tracks. "A *what*?"

Corey shook his head slowly, "Mom, you're so old fashioned."

She came back to his bedside. "You smoke that marijuana

stuff?"

"A few times. It made me hungry and kind of stupid."

Risa chuckled, "I learn something new about you every day. But no, I don't think they'd allow that."

Corey said, "I've been talking to a few of the patients in here and they swear by it. Says it makes them less nauseous from the drugs. So, I guess since they can't smoke it, they eat it."

"Eat it? In what?"

"Brownies."

"They put marijuana in brownies?"

"Mom…really…talk to Peg. She's up on all this stuff."

"Peg?"

"Yeah, she said she would ask you if she could bring me some."

Risa shook her head in silence. "Put your mask back up over your mouth, please."

He did so.

She left the room still shaking her head.

\*\*\*

At two fifty-five, Risa met Saul in the lobby. They headed to the Medical Arts building next to, and connected to the hospital through a series of hallways, elevators, and switchbacks.

Doctor Nori met them in the waiting room then ushered them into his private office. "Thank you for coming to my office—I'm seeing outpatients this afternoon. I hope it wasn't too confusing to get here. It can be daunting the first time."

Saul nodded. "It was challenging. No worse than a busy airport."

The doctor smiled. "Good." He pulled a chart in front of him and opened it. He was not smiling now. "I would like to explain the lab results for Corey. As you know, the progression of HIV can go either way. There are great days, good days, and not so good days, as you have witnessed. Barb tells me he is recovering from the therapy from yesterday. I'm sorry it had such a profoundly negative effect. The problem with the drug therapy for HIV is that we are sliding by on cancer drugs until more research is done to gear the drug directly for the immune system—which could be considered a double-edged sword. The drugs lower the fight of the immune system to irradicate the cancerous cells that are present in his lungs and lymph nodes. So, really, we are just basically running in a circle in the hopes that something catches a way out. What we need is a drug that catches the virus." He cleared his throat, moved his pen along the printed lab values on the sheet. "What we have here is a drop in the T-cells. Here we have a spike in the cancer cells. The drop in the T-cells…"

Risa stopped listening. The words, the sounds coming from Doctor Nori's mouth, the office surroundings…all blending into a nightmarish painting where the stark colors ran together without boundaries. She did not need to know the lab values because all they did was divulge how the virus and cancer were taking the lead by a landslide…that what the doctor had explained a few weeks ago regarding viral cells looking for a host—not necessarily discerning which host—but that they *had* one—came to light.

She blinked herself back to the moment and heard the following words: "We can try more rounds of anti-retroviral therapies, or we can slowly titrate him off the drugs. Keep him comfortable. He is not in any real pain right now; however, I will order a morphine regimen for that time. Let's keep him on oxygen, let him eat whatever he can tolerate, we can continue the sleeping pills as well. Let's keep the one IV going, he can be ambulatory with it." He closed the file and looked at them, his eyes gentle. "I am so very, very sorry about this recent development."

Saul stood up first and shook the doctor's hand. "Thank you, Doctor Nori. You have been exemplary. We will see you soon?"

He stood. "Of course! I'm still his attending, he might bounce back for a while. Let's just keep his spirits up."

Risa stood and nodded, "Yes. We can do that. Thank you, doctor."

As they navigated their way back to the hospital, Risa

leaned on Saul and eventually had to stop. She sat down hard in a chair and hung her head. "I can't."

Saul bent down in front of her. "I know, Reese. I know." He tried to soothe her as he held her.

She let her sobs erupt. It was her turn to crumble.

Her son was dying.

# Letters to Corey

## CHAPTER TWENTY-SIX

*MGH Oncology Unit*
*Same Day*

Risa sent Saul ahead to Corey's room so she could compose herself. She struggled with her reflection in the mirror; wasn't sure where she was going to find the energy to face her son without giving away her grief. "You can do this, Reese. Be strong for him. This is about *him*."

She peeked her head around the door to find Saul staring at his son, who was snoozing. She entered quietly and took Saul's hand. He asked in a whisper, "Feeling any better?"

"A bit. How is he? And where is Peg?"

"He was sleeping when I came in. Peg ran home to take the girls to dance practice. I was thinking of heading back to the office to tidy up a case. Would that be okay with you?"

"Of course."

Saul rose, kissed her then said, "I'll be back soon, honey."

Risa settled herself into the lounge chair next to Corey's bed—the hospital staff had graciously moved an extra one from the dialysis unit for her to use because the regular chairs were uncomfortable for long periods of time.

She closed her eyes.

***

"Mom. Mom."

Risa sat up with a start. "Wha…what?"

Corey smirked. "You were snoring."

Risa cleared her throat. "I was not! I never snore!"

Corey raised what used to be an eyebrow. "Well, you do now!" He laughed. "You must have been dreaming something fierce. You were chattering on about something or other."

"I was not!"

They looked at each other for a few seconds, then Risa said,

"Was I?"

Corey reached out for her hand. "Oh, Mom. You're not perfect, you know."

"I'm not?" She took his hand. "And here I thought all along…"

Corey said, "You look beat, Mom. Why don't you go back to the apartment and shower and change. You'll feel a lot better. Barb is here. Call me when you're ready to come back and maybe you can bring something from the deli?"

"I can do that. You're right. I could use a shower and a change of clothes."

She collected a few of her things and looked back at Corey, who was staring at her with a quizzical look on his face. "What?" She looked down at her clothes. "I know I'm a mess and—"

He cut her off. "No, you're fine." Was all he said.

She kissed him and left the room.

Corey gave his mother the requisite ten minutes to make sure she wasn't going to double back. He edged his way over on the bed, grabbed the phone and called Michael at his work. While he was on hold, he closed his eyes. His mother did not mention the conversation with the doctor; she did not have to. He knew the answers just by looking at her face.

"Corey?" Michael answered.

"Hey. So, I think you might need to come back here. Sooner than later. I think that I'm…"

"Corey, what is it? What do you think?"

"Michael," his voice caught. He cleared his throat, "I don't think I'm going to beat this."

"Core…what happened? Did the doctor talk to you?"

"Just come. Soon."

"Baby, what's happening?"

"Just…you need to be here."

Michael said quickly, "I'll re-arrange my schedule. I can probably come on Saturday."

"Okay."

"Core, did something happen?"

"Yeah. Something happened alright." He started to cry. "I was a promiscuous asshole before I met you." Tears ran down his cheeks. "Someone, I don't even know, and isn't that fucking pathetic, gave this to me." He choked on his words. His breath became more labored. "And while I was opening my heart to you, this fucking thing festered all the while…" he lowered the receiver from his mouth and sobbed "Oh, God. I can't."

"Corey? Corey! Don't hang up, baby. Stay with me here. Slow down, now. Don't get yourself upset."

He started to panic. "I feel so awful. My body…it hurts, Michael. I'm so sorry this is happening to you, to us. I feel so guilty. I can't even—" he started to cough. Hard. He sat up, gasping for air.

"Corey! Corey!" Michael called out but Corey had dropped the receiver. All Michael could hear was Corey's guttural sounds. He shouted into the phone, "Don't hang up! Get the nurse!"

Barb ran into the room, "What's—okay, okay," she sprang into action and raised his arms above his head. "Get it out, Corey. Come on, cough it out."

He struggled, gagging on his sputum. Barb grabbed the emesis basin. "You're going to be okay, just keep spitting." She kept him in an upright position while he wretched into the basin. "You're going to be okay, let's breath together, slow it down." She moved behind him with her knee supporting his back.

Another nurse entered the room. Barb called out, "Suction, stand by if he can't express the fluids. And hang up the damn phone!"

The nurse quickly hung up the phone and activated the suction unit. She gloved up, grabbed sterile packages, ripped them open then connected the hose to the wand.

Corey wheezed and gasped for air. Barb kept him steady. "He's going to pass out. Get ready. I'll hold his head."

The two worked in tandem until Corey came out of it and could breathe without vomiting. He looked at Barb, his eyes swollen, tears and mucus running down his face, his body drenched in sweat.

Barb said to the attending nurse, "Cold compress. Two." Then she said to Corey. "You're going to be okay, honey."

He hoarsely uttered, "Oh, God."

"Don't talk. You're out of the woods."

He closed his eyes and grimaced. "This time."

Barb took one compress and moved it around his face while the other nurse held one against the back of his neck. "We're here, Core. You're going to be okay."

Corey took a deep breath and let it out with an involuntary sigh. He fought the reflex to cough. He hummed as he slowed his breathing.

"Good. That's good. Just a few breaths, nice and slow." Barb breathed with him.

"I'm sorry."

"Shhh. There is nothing to apologize for."

"I know, it's your job, right?"

Barb nodded. "Damn right it is. Did someone upset you on the phone?"

"No. Oh, God, the phone!" He looked around for the receiver, "I was talking to Michael. Did I hang up on him?"

"We took the liberty."

"No, he was trying to calm me down. I told him to come to Boston as soon as he could."

"Oh?"

Corey leaned back on the upright part of the bed and closed his eyes. "Yes. He needs to come back."

Barb nodded; she understood.

## CHAPTER TWENTY-SEVEN

*MGH Oncology Unit*
*Wednesday September 30, 1981*

Risa held the job of timekeeper. Corey's new regimen consisted of two hall walks in the morning, two in the evening, and if he felt up to it, a short visit with family in the solarium. Family visits were tailored to two a day, and typically for a few hours only. And while Ruthie continued to bring in homemade goods, Risa often took most of it to the nurses. Corey's appetite had waned significantly.

Michael came, staying at the apartment while in town. He was Corey's official 'walker', while Risa stayed back in the room to tidy up. She kept his plants watered, his pillows fluffed, his clothing washed and within reach.

Alice came to the hospital to meet with Risa. They used the small conference room behind the nurse's station.

"How are you feeling this morning, Risa?"

"I don't know. Useless."

"I'm sure you're anything but useless. You are Corey's backbone right now."

Risa rolled a tissue in her palm. "I don't know, Alice. I'm mad. Frustrated."

"At?"

"Everything. There's nothing anyone can do. Nothing."

Alice nodded. "It's up to Corey's body to direct us now."

"There is something robbing me of my breath. Keeping my lungs from filling all the way or my heart from pumping."

Alice smiled thinly. "You're keeping pace with him and grief has a way of doing that to you as well."

Risa let her tears well up and drop. "When he sleeps at night I watch him. His face is so calm, even behind the oxygen mask. I think about all the wonderful experiences he and I have had together. They seem like a distant past. Alice, I'm never…" she sobbed openly.

Alice waited.

"I'm sorry, I can't even say it."

"May I share something with you?"

Risa nodded. "It would be nice to not have to talk right now."

Alice leaned forward on the table, clasping her hands together. "I know of your grief, Risa. I understand it completely."

Risa nodded, "Of course you do, you're a trained professional."

"No, I know of it firsthand."

Risa looked up, dabbing at her eyes, "What do you mean?"

"I lost my daughter when she was eight. Almost twenty years ago."

Risa stopped crying. "You what?"

"Yes. She was struck down by a drunk driver."

"Oh my God, Alice!"

"In front of our house. We lived in Somerville, then."

Risa shook her head slowly, "I didn't even know. Why haven't you said anything?"

Alice shrugged. "I don't share much of my life with my clients. And it's your hour. But the reason I bring this up today is that I understand you will not see your son's benchmarks. If Amy were still alive today, I would have watched two graduations, possibly a wedding, possibly a birth."

The enormity of the comment swirled in her head. She had thought about things she would miss but could not wrap her arms around it yet. So, she thought about Alice's daughter instead. "I can't even—oh Alice, I am so sorry for your loss."

"Thank you. So, as you can see, I am quite familiar with grief."

Risa asked quietly, "Does it ever go away?"

"No. The architecture of it stays the same, but the landscape changes over time. There isn't a day that goes by I don't think of her."

Risa gazed at a poster on the wall. A reprint of a field of flowers. "I can't even picture a future without him in it."

"Grief is another one of those objective-subjective

conditions. While we all understand what the word means, its intricacies are akin to the beholder. But also, the similarities are evident."

"Meaning?"

"Something caused, is causing, our grief. Initially for me, it was the anger at the drunk driver who struck her and the guilt that I was not on hand to pull her away from the street. What would you say it was for you?"

Risa thought about it for a moment. "Not knowing until it was too late."

"What would you have done differently?"

"I could have kept him home from school. I don't know." Risa sighed and shook her head. "I just don't know."

"I realize there is a tremendous amount on your plate right now. We can continue this dialogue when you are ready."

Risa looked back at the field of colorful flowers. "Will I ever be? Ready, that is?"

"Yes, you will. It's just going to take time."

Risa looked directly at Alice then snorted. "Time. What the hell is that?"

***

Peg insisted that Risa join her for lunch while Corey slept. Instead of going to the cafeteria, they went down to Beacon Street to a little café.

Once seated, Peg handed Risa a file folder. "I've made the arrangements with Rabbi Rothman."

"Thank you." Risa took the folder and set it down on the table. "I appreciate your leg work."

"It's not a problem. All the details are in the packet."

Risa grabbed the menu. "I'm not even hungry."

"You have to eat. Even if it's something small."

"Ruthie has been overcompensating. The nurses love her cooking. I pick at it, but I can't even taste anything."

Peg reached across the table and took Risa's hand. "Reese, you have to take care of yourself. You must stay strong."

"For what?" She looked up with pleading eyes. "My world

is completely flat, Peg. I'm barely hanging on."

"I know, honey."

"Actually; you don't. If this was reversed and I was in your shoes, I wouldn't know, either."

Peg said nothing.

Risa sighed heavily, "I'm sorry, Peg. I know you mean well. Everyone does. We all want to rally around him and maybe we think somehow that will save him. According to Alice, it's more about us—not him. It's more about our level of comfort in a situation that has nothing but darkness at the end of a tunnel. It's more about us wanting him to get better so *we* feel better."

Peg nodded. "She has a point."

"Yes. She makes many good points. Only sometimes they are so hard to hear. Sometimes I have to turn her off."

"Maybe you're not ready to hear these things yet and maybe she should have more compassion in understanding that!"

"Oh, she does. You know, she lost a daughter twenty years ago?"

"No, really?"

"A drunk driver."

"How awful!"

"So, she gets grief."

"I can't imagine."

Risa smiled mirthlessly and thought, *no, you really can't.*

## CHAPTER TWENTY-EIGHT

*MGH Oncology Unit*
*Friday October 2, 1981*

Risa and Saul watched their son rest. Doctor Nori began the morphine drip that morning.

Michael was at the apartment changing clothes. Ruthie and Abe were on their way with Rachel, and Elaine and Nathan were due to arrive later that morning.

It would be this way for two days. They would take turns in private with Corey. They would pray, hold one another, and keep the dialogue quiet. Rabbi Rothman was brought in Wednesday night to bless Corey and the family.

On Sunday October 4, 1981, Corey Joseph Shapiro, surrounded by his mother and father, twenty-seven days before his twentieth birthday, would quietly lose his life.

\*\*\*

The obituary was simple. There was no mention of his condition, just that he died peacefully surrounded by loving family. The only details included were the date and time of the memorial service and burial locations.

**"There must have been a time when you entered a room and met someone and after a while you understood that unknown to either of you there was a reason you had met. You had changed the other and he (she) had changed you. By some word or deed or just by your presence the errand had been completed. Then perhaps you were a little bewildered or humbled and grateful. And it was over. Each lifetime is the piece of a jigsaw puzzle. For some there are more pieces. For others the puzzle is more difficult to**

assemble.

Some seem to be born with a nearly completed puzzle. And so, it goes. Souls going this way and that. Trying to assemble the myriad parts.

But know this. No one has within themselves all the pieces to their puzzle. Like before the days when they used to seal jigsaw puzzles in cellophane. Ensuring that all the pieces were there.

Everyone carries with them at least one and probably many pieces to someone else's puzzle. Sometimes they know it, sometimes they don't.

And when you present your piece which may be worthless to you, to another, whether you know it or not, whether they know it or not, you are a messenger from the Most High."

Rabbi Lawrence Kushner

# CHAPTER TWENTY-NINE

*New York City*
*Wednesday February 17, 1982*
*FOUR MONTHS LATER*

"Hello, Michael? It's Risa. Mrs. Shapiro."

"Oh! Oh, my gosh. Hello!"

"I'm sorry for calling you at work but I'm in the city just overnight and I wanted to know if I could see you. Later, of course. When you are done with work."

"Oh! Well, sure. Did you want to meet for a drink?"

"I would love to see where you live!" Risa hoped she sounded nonchalant even though she felt anything but.

Michael hesitated. "Uhm, okay. I guess we could do that. Let me give you the address. Where are you staying?"

Risa lied. "Midtown."

Michael gave her the address and told her he would be home close to six o'clock. It was already four, so Risa did not have long to wait. She would sit in the lobby of the St. James and order a cocktail. When she boarded the commuter flight from Boston to New York earlier that day, she was headstrong about needing to see where Corey spent his time. She needed to feel the part of his life that did not include her.

The fifth-floor walk-up was on a brownstone lined street. Risa smelled home cooking on almost every floor. It was inviting, warm on a brisk winter night. Her heart, while thudding because of what she was about to do, felt heavy despite the anti-anxiety pills she had been taking of late.

Michael opened the door and stood on the threshold. "Mrs. Shapiro!"

Risa climbed the last steps, looked up and smiled at him. "You have facial hair!"

Michael ran his hand over his face, "Well, I thought I would try a goatee. The jury is still out. Come on in! I picked up some food from Penn Brothers. I hope you like lasagna. I didn't have time to cook."

They hugged and she entered the apartment. "Oh, please, don't go to any trouble. Lasagna will be fine!"

Michael followed her in and closed the door. "Let me take your coat. That wind is biting today!"

She unwrapped her scarf from around her neck and unbuttoned her wrap. "Thank you."

He took her outerwear down a short hall to a closet. "Why don't you make yourself comfortable in the living room? May I get you a glass of wine? As I recall, you like red."

Risa took in every inch of the surroundings. "Oh, that would be lovely. Thank you, Michael."

She heard him in the kitchen opening a bottle and pouring the wine into glasses. He called out, "The lasagna is heating up. Would you like some cheese and crackers? *That* I *do* have! Merlot okay?"

She wasn't the least bit hungry. She answered, "Merlot is fine and please, don't put yourself out. Whatever you want to do will be fine."

There were four photographs on Michael's mantel of Corey, or Corey and Michael. There he was. His million-dollar smile shining down on her.

She had to steady herself.

He entered the room, two glasses in hand. "Here we go!" He noticed her staring at the photographs and set the glasses down on coasters on a side table. "Oh. I should have—"

"Of course not." She said emphatically. She asked, "Where was this one taken?"

He stood next to her. "Fire Island. I have a friend with a place. We spent several weekends there."

Risa nodded. Several weekends…when he made excuses for not coming home over the summer. "And this one?"

"During a gay pride festival in June. Down on Christopher Street."

She noticed half-dressed men donned in leather apparel in the background of the photograph. They were all touching one another. She could feel Michael's unease.

She asked with faux enthusiasm, "And this one?"

Michael picked up the photo and held the frame gently. He nodded and sighed. "It was one of the few times I could get Corey to dress up. It was our six-month anniversary."

She turned to look at him. "Fancy dinner? Carriage ride?"

"How did you know?"

"Corey told me you were a hopeless romantic. That he had gone on a carriage ride with you after a fancy dinner." She reached down to pick up a wine glass. "Other than that, I don't know much about your relationship with him." She sipped the Merlot; it stung the back of her throat.

Michael set the picture down and grabbed his glass as well, saying nothing.

She asked, "Do you have any albums?"

Glad for the diversion, he walked toward a stereo cabinet, "Oh, sure, what's your pleasure? Jazz? Blues? Chanteuses?"

She chuckled. "Oh, not record albums; photo albums."

Michael's smile faded. "Ah." He eyed Risa. "Are you sure you want to do that, Mrs. Shapiro?"

"Yes. I'm sure."

Michael sighed, sipped his wine, then put the glass down. "I'll be right back." Then walked down the hall toward a room with a closed door.

Risa watched him hesitate then, as he reached for the doorknob, stopped. She had followed him. "Was this his room?"

"It was where he kept his things. Now it's just…"

Risa stood back, her heart trip-hammering. Something made her reach for Michael's shoulder and set her hand on it. "It's okay. We don't have to do this."

He shook his head slightly. "I don't go in very often."

Risa thought of Corey's room at home. The door was also closed. She had not been in it since he died. "I understand."

He said, "I understand why you're here. I get it."

Risa took a deep breath. "Let's do it together?"

He took a deep breath, too. "Okay."

When he opened the door, the first thing Risa was hit with was the remnant scent of Corey's cologne. When Michael flipped the light switch, she saw beige-colored walls, a small rug over the wood floors, a few framed re-production paintings on the walls, and functional furniture for a bedroom.

Michael stood looking lost. "I'm thinking of getting new furniture and turning this into an office space."

"It's a nice room, Michael. It would be perfect for an office."

He raised his arms. "All this. It's…"

They stood quietly absorbing what was left of Corey. She felt herself teeter on an emotional precipice. She reached out for Michael's hand, "Come on, let's go back to the living room. In fact, I should probably go."

Michael followed her out of the room, turning off the light and closing the door gently. "Stay for dinner?"

She said, "I think it might be best if I head back to the airport."

Michael said as he walked behind her. "I thought you were staying the night?"

"No. I'm not."

He stopped and gently reached for her shoulder. He turned her toward him and took her into his arms.

Risa stiffly returned the hug. What she wanted to do was hang on to him, feel every inch of his taut body, feel how Corey must have felt in his arms. She released him quickly.

He said softly, "I am so sorry for your loss, Mrs. Shapiro. He was very special to me for the short time I knew him."

Risa tried to speak around the lump that threatened to close her throat. She whispered, "I know, Michael. I'm glad he had you."

Michael sighed. He went toward the hall closet.

She felt small, insignificant in this man's apartment. This place where her son spent hours, days, months, in young love, in the same bed with this kind, sensitive man. Making breakfast, doing chores, dressing for an evening out, relaxing on the couch for an evening in. There she was, in the middle of their short life together feeling out of place. "Michael, I'm sorry I came. Please forgive me. I had no right to—"

He cut her off. "You had every right, Mrs. Shapiro. He was

142

your son."

She let him help her with her wraps. When she finished putting on her gloves, she looked up at him. "Thank you for loving my son. I'm sorry for your loss as well, Michael. You are a mensch."

He nodded. "Be safe."

She wasn't exactly sure where she was, but she walked, her low heels clacking on the uneven bricked surface of the sidewalk, her heart heavy, her blank mind reeling. Tears fell as she bent into the wind, throaty sighs escaping her mouth with almost every step. The darkness of the night beyond the glow of the streetlamps felt endless. She wanted to scream out loud. Passersby gave her a wide berth. She barely noticed them; the scent of his cologne embedded in her nostrils. His face in the pictures, his aura, his love; cut to the quick. He would never be again. He was truly gone.

***

She found herself back at the St. James Hotel. She asked the concierge to find her a commuter flight out of La Guardia to Boston. The last one was leaving in an hour and half. He instructed the doorman to hail her a cab.

She barely remembers the flight back or the drive north to Manchester. Her body felt like an empty cavity, nothing but muscle, sinew, and bone keeping her upright.

# Letters to Corey

# CHAPTER THIRTY

*The Office of Alice Stern*
*Monday, February 21, 1982*

She said nothing for the first fifteen minutes of the session; just looked down at the shredded tissues in her hand.

Alice waited.

Finally, Risa looked up. "I went to New York City."

"Oh? To pick up Corey's belongings?"

"No." She sighed heavily. "No. I went to see Michael. At his apartment. But as it turned out, that was a mistake."

"What was the mistake?"

Risa put her head back onto the couch. "I shouldn't have gone there. It was as if I stepped into something that wasn't mine to step in."

"Something sacred, perhaps?"

"Yes. This whole world…where I never belonged."

"A world that you were not privy to."

Risa whispered, "The truth hurts so much, Alice."

"There is no easy way to understand this, I'm afraid."

"No, there isn't."

Alice took off her glasses. "Imagine an invisible line between when our children are truly children, and then when they transition into young adulthood. It typically happens in their late teens. Especially with boys. In a normal situation, you'd be dealing with expected things that boys-to-men can get themselves into. For example: puberty, dating, school, scuffles with friends, that sort of thing. In your case, your son was different because of his sexuality; bringing with it an entirely different set of rules and regulations. As I recall, you had asked him to keep his private life outside of the boundaries of your home and town. And we must credit him for complying with that. But the downside meant you weren't included in his life experiences outside those boundaries. And not from any fault of yours, you asked him to be respectful. Which is perfectly right and normal. And keep in mind," she leaned forward and added, "that the entire situation might have blossomed over a period of time."

Risa added, "Only, we did not have that kind of time."

"No, unfortunately you did not."

Risa was quiet for a moment then said, "I feel at fault. For making him keep it separate."

"You are not at fault. You were forthright because of extenuating circumstances at home."

"Right. Homosexuality. A disease unto itself. Better not let the neighbors know." Her voice was acerbic.

"Is that how you really feel?"

"I don't know what in the hell I feel. All I can do is cry and take Valium—which I hate by the way. I'm not a pill popper."

"They work well in the short term but can be habit forming."

"I know, I've been warned."

Alice said, "Remember the seven stages of grief. You've got to give yourself time to experience those."

"Yeah. Where am I now? The anger stage, the guilt stage? Certainly not the denial stage!"

"The stages, while universal, are quite subjective."

"Well." She leaned her arms on her thighs, snapping another tissue out of the box. "I seem to not feel anything. I just cry."

"Crying is a good, normal release. You're certainly feeling things."

"But I feel numb inside. So much chaos in my head. I can't make heads or tails of it."

Alice said, "Risa, you must give yourself time to acclimate. Your life before all of this was smooth and natural. You had an order, substance. And then caretaking became your new normal."

"I never in my *life* expected to endure this."

"Most people don't. And when it strikes, it strikes with fury."

Risa looked at her. "Yes, you know that very well, too."

"I do." Alice stood up and pulled a small package from a brown paper bag that was on her desk. "Risa, I wanted to give you something. Maybe something that will help."

Risa took it and looked at Alice, "What is this?"

"Just open it."

She pulled off the paper and looked at a small leatherbound book. When she opened the pages, they were blank. She looked up at Alice with an unspoken question.

Alice explained, "When Amy died, my therapist at the time suggested I start a journal. Write down anything or everything. It mattered not."

"A diary?" Risa almost laughed.

"Yes, a journal. Just for you, no one else's eyes unless you want to share what you write, a place for you to put your feelings, thoughts, whatever. I used to write letters to Amy, and it helped me connect with her. I still do on occasion!"

Risa handled the soft leather in her hands and studied it. "It's beautiful, really. The paper is so smooth."

"I find a cartridge pen works the best."

Risa said, "I can't take this from you. I mean, it's so thoughtful, but you don't have to buy me things."

"I thought you might like to have it with you. In your purse, or at home at your desk. It might really help when you have no one to talk to or just don't feel like talking to anyone. Might help you sort out the chaos in your head. It worked for me."

Risa looked off. "I had a diary as a kid. It had a lock and key. I wrote about the boys I liked. My friends had their own and sometimes during sleepovers we'd share our deepest secrets." She snorted. "Deepest secrets…Lord."

Alice chuckled along with her. "So, what do you think, want to give it try?"

"Letters, hmm? How did that work out for you?"

"It was cathartic. It brought me closer to her."

"Do you still write? In a journal?"

"I do. Maybe not as frequently. But I continue to, yes."

Risa sighed. "It's really lovely. Thank you."

"Perhaps it would serve you well to write from the gut and not worry about grammar or if any of it makes sense. If it makes sense to you, that's all that counts."

"Maybe it *will* work."

When she left Alice's office, she had a new focus. Something to anchor her instead of aimless grief.

Her next stop was to the stationary store in town. She would need a nice fountain pen.

To hell with Valium.

THERAPY NOTE:
*Concerns: Acute stage of denial of which she denies; panic searching for answers i.e., trip to NYC to meet with Michael- which turned out disappointing, proof that her son lived a life she was not included in; searching for panacea, suggested journaling. I sense a breakdown could possibly occur within the first year of grieving, there will be a variety of triggers. AS*

\*\*\*

**JOURNAL ENTRY**
**Monday February 21, 1982**

*Dearest Corey,*

*My sweet son. Alice gave me this beautiful journal. I went to Bromfield to find just the right pen. So here I am. Alice thought it would be a good thing. For me to write…about you, about me, about life I guess. Where to start?*

*Maybe I should just say that I miss you so. How could I not? I see you everywhere…*

*I'm not sure how to do this—it's been since I was a teenager! I had a lock and key diary where I kept my most private thoughts. Hah! You would laugh. About boys, teachers I didn't like, that sort of thing. Otherwise, my life was pretty much run of the mill. We had a crazy household with dad always traveling with the orchestra and mom and us girls running things while he was away.*

*Who am I kidding. I am miserable. I haven't gone into your room yet. The door is still shut. Your things from the hospital are still in a bag in the basement. Dad washed them. We still have to go to New York to collect your belongings. I don't think I can*

go. I went to see Michael. It was a mistake. You had a life with him without me. I am hurt by that. Why? Why couldn't you tell us about him? You looked happy. In the pictures.
  You shut me out.
  I don't think I can do this.
  Your loving mom.

***

## JOURNAL ENTRY
## Tuesday February 22, 1982

  My son,
  I'm going to try this again. I could barely get out of bed today. It's cold and rainy, the trees are bare, dripping. Your dad is at work, Rachel at school. The house is too quiet. I can't really eat anything yet; it all gets stuck somewhere between my shoulders. It feels like I can't get in a deep breath. Is this what it felt like for you? Really. I'm so tired.
  That's all for now.
  Your loving mom

***

## JOURNAL ENTRY
## Wednesday February 23, 1982

  My darling Corey,
  The sun is out today, the sky is crystal clear blue. I slept okay last night. Soundly, don't remember my dreams. Which is a good thing because of late they have been frustrating—where I'm supposed to be somewhere, and I can't get there, and people are depending on me. And no matter how hard I try to get where I'm supposed to be, I keep ending up back where I started.
  My heart still beats although I'm not sure how.
  Your loving mom

***

**JOURNAL ENTRY**
**Thursday February 24, 1982**

*Hello my dearest Corey,*

*Well, I ventured out today. Went to Filene's. Saw Claire, our favorite make-up technician. She tried some new things on my face—she's always calm and wonderful, so I let her create. Mrs. Armistead came out from behind the counter and told me I look beautiful. Oh Corey...the make-up was nothing new or exciting, just re-arranged. Claire packaged all my new cosmetics up in a lovely powder blue bag with silk handles. She gave me a hug with an extra squeeze.*

*So, I went to the clothing department and picked out things you would probably think weren't classy enough. I was in the dressing room, and I just couldn't do it, Core. I sat down on the bench and cried. Made a mess of the new make-up...I used my sunglasses cleaning cloth in an attempt to blot it, but I only succeeded to make it blotchier. I left the clothes on the hangers, piled other clothes on the bench, and left the little blue bag with all the nice cosmetics for some other woman—pay it forward, you used to say.*

*On my way out of the mall, I heard a father tell his son that black tape would fix the crack in his toy fire engine. That black tape fixes everything.*

*I drove to the little hardware store north of town and bought ten rolls of black tape. The clerk at the front counter blathered on incessantly about the virtues of black tape and commented on the amount I was buying—that my <u>husband</u> must have some big project he's working on! I almost slapped him. When I left the store, I dumped the bag of tape in the garbage can outside the door and the clerk ran after me yelling 'don't' you want your tape, lady? Hey lady!' Instead, I gunned the engine out of the parking lot and stopped half-way home on a back road and, of course, sobbed.*

*How could that man at the mall lie to his son about black tape fixing everything? I want to find him and tell him that black tape does NOT fix everything. Not the lesions, not the destroyed*

*lungs, not the bulging lymph nodes. NO!*
    *How am I going to get through this, Corey?*
    *Your loving mom*

***

**JOURNAL ENTRY**
**Friday February 25, 1982**

    *My dear sweet love,*
    *My heart just aches.*
    *That is all.*
    *Love,*
    *Mom*

# Letters to Corey

## CHAPTER THIRTY-ONE

*Manchester*
*Saturday February 26, 1982*

For Rachel's seventeenth birthday, Peg organized a surprise party at the country club: A buffet dinner followed by dancing, the music provided by a local rock band. Risa and Saul paid for it, Risa did what she could to help set it up, but otherwise left most of it up to Peg.

The plan was to get Rachel to the country club under the guise of meeting the grandparents for dinner.

In her dressing area, Risa sat on her fabric bench and stared at her clothing. Saul was already dressed and waiting for her downstairs.

"Reese?" he called from the bottom of the steps. "You almost ready?"

She grunted.

"Reese?"

When she didn't answer him a second time, he came up the steps. At the threshold of her dressing room, he said, "Honey? Are you okay?"

"I'm... fine. Just deciding what pair of shoes to wear." She looked down at her feet.

He went to her. "Honey, I think once you're out and about, you'll feel a lot better, don't you think?" He took her gently by the chin. "This is for Rachel. Let's not let her down?"

Risa turned her face away from his hand. "I won't. Just give me a minute, alright?"

He stood back. "Okay, which dress are you thinking of wearing?"

She put her hands on the bench and looked away from him. "Can you just give me a few minutes, please?"

"We have to be there at a certain time. It's a—"

She cut him off sharply. "I *know* it's a surprise, Saul. I'll be down in a few minutes, *okay*?!"

Saul backed out. "Okay, okay. Rachel is warming up the car."

Risa nodded then looked back at her wardrobe. She waited until Saul went downstairs. "What dress, Core? Not black. It's too somber for such a glorious occasion. How about the pink number? What, you think it's too gaudy? Beige suit, maybe? Oh, too matronly. Okay, navy blue. That always works. Now, which shoes…"

She bent down and picked up a pair of low heels.

It took her another five minutes to pull it together, then she went downstairs, where Saul was waiting with her overcoat, scarf, and gloves over his arm. When he saw her, he smiled, "There's my beautiful girl."

Risa smiled appropriately then allowed Saul to help her with her garments. She fought the urge to tell him she would rather just stay home and write in her journal because she wanted to be close to Corey.

He took her hand, "Shall we?"

She walked with him to the car.

*\*\*\**

"She's having a great time with her friends. So good to see her smile and laugh." Ruthie said to Risa. "Are you enjoying yourself, honey?"

"Oh, sure!" She reached for her wine glass.

Saul looked at her. "Easy does it, Reese. You're a lightweight."

Risa snorted and took a long swallow of the wine. When the glass was empty, she set it down and regarded her husband. "Well, honey, it seems to be going down just fine. I'm fine. Maybe I'm not such a lightweight after all." She grabbed the bottle.

Ruthie signaled Saul to leave the table.

He caught on, pushed his chair back, and stood up. "Well, maybe my daughter would like to dance with her old man."

Risa guffawed as she poured unsteadily. "Oh? When was the last time *you* cut a rug? And to rock music?"

Saul cocked his head. "I believe it was at Corey's graduation party." He went looking for Rachel.

Risa glared at his back as he wended his way through the crowd.

Ruthie noticed. "Honey, easy."

"Oh, mother," she turned to look at her. "Really! He just threw that in my face! How dare he?"

"What? What did he throw in your face? You asked him a question and he answered you. Wha—"

"Corey's graduation party. Stab, *stab*!"

Ruthie held Risa's hand that held the wine glass. "Stop. Stop this right now."

"What? Stop what? Aren't I entitled to have feelings?" She pulled her wrist from her mother's hand and drank.

"Of course, you are."

"He seems to be over the loss of his son."

Ruthie said incredulously, "How could you say such a thing?"

"Look at him." Her glare went to the dance floor where he was swinging his arms around while his daughter laughed with him. "He's making a complete jackass out of himself!"

"He's *enjoying* himself! Let him be!"

No one else seemed to notice Saul on the dance floor but Risa was getting more annoyed by the moment. "Mom, why don't you go find dad? I'm fine here."

Ruthie shook her head. "You know, the only other time I've seen you this abrasive was when you had post-partum depression. That was twenty years ago."

"Well obviously you don't live at our house. Couples fight, you know."

"This isn't fighting, Reese, this is blatant disrespect. You know better than this. Either that or you're drunk."

Risa turned to face her mother with a thin smile on her lips. "And what if I am? Drunk? Maybe this is my way of coping. I'm tired of feeling, tired of crying. How about that, Mom? Your prized eldest daughter has flaws!"

Ruthie stood up. "I don't need to listen to this anymore."

Risa jiggled her shoulders. "Suit yourself."

Risa sat alone at the table.
She wished she had brought her journal.
Corey would understand.

## CHAPTER THIRTY-TWO

Banging. She willed it to stop, yelled for it to stop, screamed at the top of her lungs for it to stop but to no avail. It kept coming, steady and strong. She ran from room to room, but the sound followed her.

"Risa!"

She jolted awake only to see her husband's face just a foot from hers. "What?" she croaked, turning away from him.

"You were having a nightmare."

She lay perfectly still to calm the nausea threatening in her throat. She knew immediately where the banging sound originated. It was from the throbbing in her temples and back of the head. She moaned. "I'm going to be sick."

He got a trash can in the nick of time.

When she was done, he set the can in the bathroom and soaked a washcloth in cool water.

She put her hand over her eyes. "Oh, God. What in the hell…"

Saul gently patted her face and neck, cleaned up her mouth. "You tied a good one on, Reese. I don't think I've ever seen you that drunk."

She slowly shook her head. "Remember that cast party several years ago? You and I had words before the guests arrived and I decided to drown our argument in mixed drinks."

"Yes, I recall. That was a good one, too, you're right."

She stretched her limbs. "I feel like I got hit by a truck."

"No doubt."

"What time is it?"

"Almost ten o'clock."

"I feel like I could sleep all day. Where is Rachel?"

"She's in her room, sleeping I imagine."

"Did she have fun last night?"

"I believe she did. But, Reese, I might as well warn you, she's pretty upset with you."

"With me? Why?"

"You were quite drunk. You said some things that offended her."

Risa sat up a bit, got dizzy, then steadied herself, "Whoa. Give me a minute." She closed her eyes and tried to breathe normally. She asked, "What did I say?"

"You might want to discuss it with her."

"Okay, I will. Let me get myself together before that, though. I hope I didn't make a complete ass out of myself."

Saul just shrugged.

She said, "I did, didn't I?"

The phone rang next to the bed. Saul picked up the receiver. "Hello? Oh, hi Ruthie. She's okay. A little worse for the wear but—"

Risa mouthed to Saul, "I'll call her back later."

He continued, "She'll get back to you when she's composed herself. Okay, love you too." He hung up then went into the bathroom to clean up the can.

"Can you get me some aspirin, please?"

He called out, "In a minute."

She tried to remember what happened after the dinner service was over and the dancing began. She recalled a few conversations with her mother and Saul but that was it.

As was routine, her now-coherent mind shifted to thoughts of Corey.

She closed her eyes.

***

Risa knocked on Rachel's door.
"Who is it?"
"Mom."
"Oh."
"Can I come in?"
"Maybe later."
"Rachel, please. Let me in. I want to talk to you."
"Well, maybe I don't want to talk to you."
"Rachel, honey. Please."
Rachel unlocked the door and opened it just a crack. She

said, "What, Mom?"

"May I come in, at least?"

Rachel stepped back, opened the door wider for her to enter, and sighed. "I'm kind of tired. Can we make it quick?" Risa sat down on the edge of Rachel's bed; Rachel chose to sit in her desk chair. "So, talk."

"I don't have to tell you I got soused last night. I don't remember what I said or did, but I want to apologize in advance."

Rachel looked directly at her mother. "Yeah, you said some pretty awful things, Mom. And I just don't know if I can forgive you."

"Honey, what did I say? You know I would never hurt you."

"The experts say people say things when they're drunk because they are completely uninhibited. But the thoughts are always there; just hidden. So, they must be true."

"Now wait a minute. What did I say?"

Rachel looked away, tears forming around her eyes. "I don't even know if I can…"

Risa reached out to her, but she backed away with her palm out. "No, don't. He was my brother!" her voice rose exponentially. "You aren't the only one who is having a hard time, but no, you can't seem to see beyond your own pain to see anyone else's!"

Risa put her hand to her heart. "Rachel, no! I—"

Rachel stood up and pointed a finger at her mother. "You don't always get to be the one in pain, Mother! There are many of us suffering just like you. But you get to take center stage, as always!" Her tears flowed through her anger. "Always the leading lady, right? Always the center of attention!"

Risa sat dumbstruck. She had never heard her daughter speak like this. To anyone.

Rachel continued. "When Corey was sick you were like the time police, letting us see him for only a few minutes! You took control of everything! Even the obituary, saying how he was surrounded by his loving family. It was just you and dad! How could you even know how we felt? Wasn't it bad enough that we were *all* robbed of Corey's life, but in the end, we couldn't even see him! You wanted him all to yourself. You always have! He was your true love, wasn't he? Not even dad had your heart the way he did!"

Risa put her hand to her mouth, stifling a sob and wishing Rachel's words to be retracted. She had no shield for this; it was so unexpected. She felt the walls closing in.

Rachel stood, out of breath, her face beet red, leaning her body awkwardly toward her mother. "I don't even understand you half the time. You're always so busy making things perfect when they never really are! It's like you live on another planet."

Risa looked up to her daughter and whispered, "Rachel, I never knew you felt this way."

"How could you? *When* have you ever spent the kind of time with *me* that you spent with Corey? I'll bet you knew him inside and out."

Risa shook her head slowly. "No, Rachel. I don't think I really knew him."

Rachel grabbed a tissue from the box. "Oh, sure. How could that be?"

Risa sighed deeply. "He led two lives. I was not privy to his other one."

Rachel started in again, "Well, do you blame him? You and dad were so worried about what people would say if they knew he was gay. And worse, that he contracted the gay plague! And dad, it's no secret what he thinks of gay people. Corey confided in me a long time ago that he thought he was different, but he made me promise *not* to tell you and dad. I kept my promise! I knew more about him than you or dad did, until you caught him, that is."

Risa was still in shock. Her children had bonded right in front of her face, and she was completely blind to it. She stood. "Rachel, I don't know what to say but suffice it to say, I am sorry. I never meant to hurt you." She tried to approach her, but Rachel stepped away.

"All I can say is I can't wait to leave this fucking mad house for college."

"Rachel! How dare you—"

Rachel turned on her heel, went into her bathroom, and slammed the door.

# Letters to Corey

## CHAPTER THIRTY-THREE

She wasn't sure how she found her way back to the master suite, but when Saul came out of the bathroom after his shower, he went directly to her. "Risa! Are you okay?"

She shook her head slowly, unable to speak. He sat down beside her on the bed; a towel wrapped around his waist. She stared off into the space of the room. He asked, "What happened with Rachel?"

She finally said, "Saul, I think I need to get out of here."

"Out of here? What does that mean?"

"I need to be out of this house, away from here."

"From Rachel and I?"

"That too."

He nodded slowly, considering her words. "So, you want to move? Sell the house, go on a trip somewhere? What?"

"A trip. Somewhere far away from here. Alone."

He put his arm around her. She did not respond. "Okay. Can you help me understand why?"

"If you don't know by now…"

"You're grieving, Reese. Obviously. Have you discussed this with Alice?"

"What," she said sharply, "do I need Alice's approval?"

"No. But they say—"

She cut him off, "I *know* what they say, Saul. But *they* are not *me*!"

He looked away from her. "Risa, we are all struggling with this. Grieving. Why can't we do this together, like a family?"

"Because right now, we are not a family. Rachel hates me."

"Oh, honey, she doesn't hate you. She's just—"

Risa stood up suddenly, Saul's arm flopping to the bed. "No! She's just—nothing! She's accusing me of things I never knew she felt and frankly, I don't have the strength to dispute those accusations. Short of being a shitty mother to her, I failed my son!"

Saul stood and turned her to face him. "You did *not* fail our son. No way! He lived a lifestyle that had terrible consequences. Nobody's fault. And if Rachel is accusing you of being a shitty mother, you must talk this out with her."

Risa pursed her lips. "Do you know she can't wait to get out of this fucking madhouse to go to school?"

Saul's eyebrows rose, "Did she really say that?"

"Yes, she did!"

He rubbed the stubble on his chin, "Hmph. I'll have to talk to her about that. That wasn't fair."

"Fair? How about it's the goddamned truth?! How about that?"

Saul started back into the bathroom to find his robe. "I'll go talk to her right now."

Risa stopped him. "Don't. You don't have to do my bidding for me. I'll get with her later. Right now, all I want to do is soak in a tub and get rid of this hangover. Then, I'm going to call Stan Keller and make arrangements for travel."

"Where are you thinking of going, Risa?"

"I don't know yet. Somewhere far away from here."

Saul shook his head. "It's a shame you feel you have to run away from us. We are not the enemy here."

Risa walked right past him, went into the adjoining bathroom, and did as her daughter did to her.

She slammed the door.

## CHAPTER THIRTY-FOUR

*The Office of Alice Stern*
*Wednesday March 3, 1982*

Alice shook her head, "I don't think it's a good idea, Risa."

"I don't really care what you think at this point, Alice," she said, exasperated. "I've got to go."

If Alice was offended by the comment, she did not show it. "I understand the need to flee, especially on the heels of what your daughter said to you, but it could very well backfire on you. This could be just a quick fix and then what?"

"Who made up these rules? Who said grieving must be this way or the highway? Many people travel, I'm sure, when tragedy strikes!"

"Perhaps, but not typically alone. To another country."

"I'm going somewhere I've already been and fell in love with. Saul and I went to Florence for our honeymoon. It just feels right. I can't explain it."

Alice leaned forward in her chair. "I'm concerned that with this trip, you might think you'll move through your pain easier. Perhaps you think a change of the landscape might jog your heart, give you a breath of fresh air."

"And what is wrong with that?"

"What is wrong is that it is temporary. You still must come home and face what you left behind."

"But don't you think if I can get a different perspective, I can deal with home better?"

Alice nodded, "Perhaps. But Risa, you're not that evolved yet. It's been less than six months since Corey's passing. Maybe seven by the time you go."

"Well, what about you? You said you moved away quickly after Amy died. I'm not leaving until May. Wasn't that, as you say, a quick fix too?"

She nodded, "It could be seen that way, but it was gradual. It took us a year to find a place, pack up and sell. It was a mutual decision that my husband and I made. She was killed right out in front of our house."

Risa shook her head. "A travesty, indeed. But I just need to get away from everyone and everything. I need a different perspective."

"I can appreciate that. I'm glad you're giving it another few months before you go."

"So, why aren't you giving me your blessing?"

"Do you really need my blessing? You said you weren't looking for advice. If you go and things turn out in your favor, then you've accomplished the next step in your grieving process. If not, and you return to the way you left, what will you have achieved? The choice is ultimately yours. Not mine, not Saul's not anyone's."

Risa looked away from her. "I can't explain. I think it's what Corey would want me to do."

THERAPY NOTE:
*I am very concerned/Risa's travel plans. Obsession with her son and what he would think of her actions, see notes RE argument with daughter. AS*

***

**JOURNAL ENTRY**
*Friday March 5, 1982*

*Hello, my dear sweet Corey,*
*Well, I managed to achieve a truce with your sister. She's so angry and hurt. She misses you terribly. She blames me and dad for a lot of what went on but mostly me because she feels I was closer to you than her. My mother always told me the first born is typically the special one. And you certainly were. Are. Were. No, are.*
*She's going to Harvard next year.*
*Then it'll be just your dad and me in this big old house.*

*I'm going to Europe in May.*
*Back to Italy, to Florence.*
*I had hoped to get back there as a family when Rachel graduated high school. But it's just going to be me. Your dad is not happy I am traveling all that way alone. But I have to do it, Core. I have to do it...I can hear your voice: 'Go for it, Mom! You only live once!'*
*He wants me to stay at a big hotel. But instead, I chose a family-owned Inn on the Arno River near the Ponte Vecchio. Why go to Europe and experience an Americanized hotel when you can go for the real thing? It's called the Inn Firenze, family owned by the Giancarlo's. It looks positively charming. It's named after the capital of Tuscany. Just a three-story colorful, old building that does not have elevator service.*
*The trip is giving me focus, honey. I am excited and nervous. Of course, Pegleg and Black Pearl will come with me. You will come with me. You're always with me.*
*In two months, I will be flying to Rome. Wednesday May 5$^{th}$.*
*Until then, I will do my best to keep my head up.*
*I love you with all my heart, son.*
*Your mom*

***

## JOURNAL ENTRY
### Sunday March 7, 1982

*My Corey,*
*I miss you terribly today. The sun is out, the temperature is unseasonable warm. I'm going to go walk on the beach. I like to let the sea air wash through me. It will be a welcome change from the ice-cold air that is Cape Ann in the winter. But alas, not to last long...a snowstorm is predicted for tomorrow overnight. A nor'easter. Your dad is going to pull wood in from the garage and build us a fire. Like old times. Remember the night we lost power and slept in the living room near the fire? We all played games while your dad fed the fire. I think you were seven. Rachel thought it was the coolest thing. We were so*

*close...when did we stray. You and I?*

*Rachel has a new beau. His name is Jeffrey. You went to school with his brother, Daniel. The Dubers. They're a nice family. Jeffrey is a senior as well, heading to Princeton in the Fall.*

*I feel as though I am rambling on about nothing at all. But this is my life right now. I'm not doing any theatre—just not in the right space for it. I clean the house, do the grocery shopping, take care of things for your father and sister. Every two weeks we go to Ruthie and Abe's for dinner. Just your dad and I. Rachel is always welcome—she joins us occasionally. Then once a month we endure Elaine and Nathan. It's family. Rachel does not attend, and I can't say I blame her. Peg drags me out for drinks and gossip—or rather she calls it discussion. I go. I endure. But it's forced. Alice says I should just go and keep going, even if it is forced. Eventually, it won't be forced, I suppose.*

*Honey...I can't stand how much I miss you. And there is nothing I can do to stop it. You won't materialize someday and say, 'Fooled ya!'. No, you won't do that at all. I wish you could, though. I wouldn't even be mad. I would just hold you and hold you and hold you. And maybe I'll write something to you of substance soon. I'm sorry I'm so sad...*

*Your loving mom*

## CHAPTER THIRTY-FIVE

*10:00 PM*
*Two Months Later*
*Wednesday May 5, 1982*
*Boston Logan Airport, International Concourse*

"Alitalia flight six forty-three departing for Rome, Italy is now ready to board passengers holding tickets for first class at gate 24."

Risa clutched Saul's hands. "It's really happening, Saul."

He smiled and kissed her lips softly, "I'll miss you, Reese."

She hugged him hard. "You have been such a mensch these past few months. I don't know how you put up with me."

He held her close to him. "You just travel safe and come home to us in three weeks."

She closed her eyes. "I will, honey. I will."

She backed away, quickly running her fingers along his forehead, "You need a haircut."

He laughed. "Only you, Reese. Only you. I promise, I'll be clean shaven and cut close by the time you get home."

She kissed him on the lips. "You are my rock, Saul. I don't know how you do it, but you are my rock."

He tilted his head. "We all grieve differently. I'm not out of the woods, yet."

"I know, honey." She hugged him again. "Okay. Well. I'm off to the Inn Firenze. I will call you when I get to Rome."

"Safe travels, honey. I love you."

"I love you, too."

She turned and joined the other first-class passengers waiting to board the plane. She couldn't believe this day had finally arrived.

She was ready for this departure and hoped it would turn out the way she needed it to—that she would sightsee, eat leisurely, not think about home but send postcards, adventure in the splendor of Italy, and give herself the opportunity to feel anything else but laden with grief. She felt an excitement she hadn't felt in a very long time, so she thought this was a good sign.

## CHAPTER THIRTY-SIX

*The Inn Firenze*
*Florence, Italy*
*Thursday May 6, 1982*

The Inn was just as she pictured it. The photographs in the brochure only told half the story; it was the scent and atmosphere that completed the experience. She stepped into the lobby, closing her eyes, breathing in the slightly musty yet homey feel. She knew she had made the right choice.

Mrs. Bertella Giancarlo, the proprietor, was a heavy-set yet sturdy woman with brilliant blue eyes, graying hair tied back into a bun with stray strands framing her kind face. She called out from behind the reception desk where she stood, "Welcome to the Inn Firenze! You must be Mrs. Shapiro!" She pronounced it *Shapperow* and Risa didn't have the heart to correct her. She thought it was sweet.

Risa smiled and approached the desk. "Yes! Hello! And please, call me Risa."

Mrs. Giancarlo nodded, "Of course, such a beautiful name, Risa." She pronounced it *Rayeesa*, and again, Risa hadn't the heart to correct her. "And you will call me Bertie. *Everyone* now calls me Bertie. My son-in-law, he doesn't call me momma anymore, he calls me Bertie!" Her laughter filled the small, quaint lobby with its aged wood and chipped marble appointments.

"Such a beautiful place, Bertie. I'm so glad to be here." Risa liked Bertie immediately. She thought she was as genuine as they get.

Once the check-in was complete, Bertie said, "Come, I will take you to your room. It's just up the stairs here, on the second floor. You will have a great view of the beautiful Arno." She grabbed Risa's two suitcases.

Risa protested, "Oh, really, I can certainly take—"

"Here we go!" She led the way.

The small, well-appointed room on the second floor had a canopy bed, a tall armoire, a small desk and chair, a bedside lamp and table, and a bathroom next to the armoire. Bertie quickly opened the bay windows. "Let's get some fresh breeze off the river. Such a beautiful day in Florence today, no?"

Risa nodded. "Gorgeous."

Bertie made sure there were fresh linens in the bathroom. "You come all the way from Boston! We have family right there in town. Such a beautiful city, Boston is."

Bertie gave Risa the room key and said, "We have wine and fresh cheese and bread every day on the patio by five o'clock. You must come down! Well, to be truthful, you and two others are here this week. By the end of the weekend, it will be more! You'll join us?"

Risa smiled and nodded, "Of course I will. It sounds lovely."

After Bertie left the room, Risa stood in the middle of what would be her home for the next three weeks. It was charming, with its slightly slanted worn wide wood plank floors, it's simple yet tasteful furnishings, and a few photographs placed here and there of Tuscany on the cream-colored textured walls. The two windows had a ledge so she could sit and look out. Indeed, the view was just as she thought it would be. Bustling and alive.

She unpacked, setting up the room just so: the framed family photo from the mantel at home was placed, along with her journal, and pen on the desk, she assembled her toiletries on the small shelf under the bathroom mirror, hung her clothes in the armoire, put her other garments in the drawers in the armoire, and stowed her suitcases in the corner.

She needed a shower first and foremost, then she was going to venture out to a café.

She was ravenous.

Something she hadn't felt in seven months.

***

The Piazza Della Signoria was bustling with late afternoon activity. Risa felt the hum of the many dialects spoken between the street vendors and performers, musicians, and voices coming from behind open windows in the marketplace. It was just as she remembered it: the historic architecture and cobble-stoned streets, the neon signs and small cafés, the churches in the distance; their steeples cutting into an azure blue sky, all quenched her thirsty soul. She smiled as she walked.

Something else she hadn't felt in seven months.

After purchasing post cards from a small shop, she made her way to the Trattoria Rosalia—a recommendation from Bertie—and sat down at a small outside table for two. Setting her purse on one chair and post cards and pen next to her, she perused the menu.

A handsome young waiter approached "Good afternoon, Signora, what would you like for today?"

She ordered a bottle of San Pellegrino, an antipasti plate, and a glass of Pinot Grigio—highly suggested by the waiter who spoke enough broken English to be understood.

She sat back, allowing the atmosphere to transform her. It could not have been more perfect. Here she was, thousands of miles away from home, in a country she adored, around people who seemed like they hadn't had a care in the world. She allowed the newness of her surroundings to quell any fears about traveling alone she'd had along the way. Even Bertie was impressed she was without her husband.

The finochia and Panzanella were delicious, the wine relaxing her shoulders from the travels of the last day and a half. She took her time eating, stopping every so often to jot a note on one of the postcards.

A young couple approached the café.

Risa froze, her fork poised mid-air, and did a double take. The man was a dead-ringer for Corey: clean-shaven, tall, dark features with his wavy hair flopped over his forehead, deep-set green eyes, and when he laughed with his female companion at something she said, Risa could barely swallow. His smile was identical.

The couple was seated to her right, the man's profile in her sightline. Even his gestures were similar; long tapered fingers on the menu, the way he sat back in his chair crossing his long slim legs leisurely over the knee, and the way he gestured to his companion with ease.

She set her fork down, feeling lightheaded. This was not something she had remotely prepared for; seeing someone who resembled her son. It caught her off guard.

She tried to divert her attention back to her postcards, but they were a blur to her now on the table, as was the food. Her appetite immediately waned, and she pushed the plate off to the side, half eaten.

Panic crept into her chest. *No, don't panic, you're alright.*

Her gentle surroundings now became a source of loud noises, too much color, too much activity. It was as if a run-away train came to a sudden halt in her chest. *Oh, God. Leave! Now!*

She stood up unsteadily, grabbed her wallet from her purse, took out enough money to cover the meal, then scurried away from the table.

She heard the waiter call after her, "Signore, Signore! Your postcards!"

Risa blindly made her way back toward the Inn, stopping every few minutes to shake the dizziness from her head and to breathe against the nausea threatening in the back of her throat. She tripped every once in a while on the uneven cobblestones, her big purse weighing her down.

People who passed her on the street gave her a wide berth. Someone mumbled, "Too much vino!"

When she arrived at the Inn, she stumbled up the stairs, barely got her key in the door, and once inside, ran to the bathroom.

***

The room was dark when she woke up. She had no idea where she was. Still in her clothes on top of the bedcovers, her mouth felt pasty and sour.

She sat up slowly, the afternoon's events crawling back into her consciousness. She swung her legs over the side of the bed; the customary dark ache found its way back to her soul.

"Who am I kidding?" she lowered her head, tears plopping

onto her wrinkled slacks. "I need to go home."

Her body shook as if she had chills. She felt sick. Empty. Defeated. Scared.

An odd sound shocked her out of her episode. It was coming from the telephone on the small nightstand next to the bed. Two quick chirps then a pause, then another two quick chirps.

She picked up the receiver. "Hello?" She absently sniffed.

The operator said, "I have a person-to-person call for Risa Shapiro from Saul Shapiro."

"Yes, this is Risa."

"Go ahead, sir."

His voice sounded so far away. "Risa? Is everything okay? I was worried when I didn't hear from you at the appointed time."

Risa took a deep breath. She was about to tell him what happened at the café but stopped herself. The whole purpose of the trip—the very expensive trip—was to detach from her broken record of despair. She quickly recovered. "I must be more jet-lagged than I thought. I fell asleep earlier and must have slept right through." The clock on the nightstand read nine-fifteen. It was three-fifteen in Manchester. She was supposed to call him at six o'clock at her time.

"Are you alright, though? You sound like you have a cold. You aren't getting sick, are you?"

Risa's head felt clogged. "The phone woke me up. The time change has me all discombobulated."

"Okay," he hesitated, "you just sound very off."

"I'm so—" she stopped herself. *Don't do it*! "I'm just tired. I promise I'll call you tomorrow.

"Okay. I love you, honey."

"I love you too."

She replaced the receiver back into the cradle and sat still. Sounds from the street below filtered in through the open windows. A cool breeze filled the room.

She felt adrift again.

The afternoon had blindsided her.

She realized she was dehydrated but did not want to drink the water from the tap. Bertie told her when she checked in she was welcome to the amenities from the Inn kitchen after hours—like water, milk, wine.

She left her room and padded down the steps to the lobby which was thankfully empty. The kitchen was off a short corridor next to the reception desk.

She went to the refrigerator, found an unopened bottle of San Pellegrino, took a glass from a cupboard, then went stealthily back toward the lobby.

Risa had hoped she could get back upstairs unnoticed. But Bertie was at the front desk.

Bertie called out, "Ah! Mrs. Shapiro, we missed you today on the patio!"

Risa stammered, "Yes, well, I had lunch at the café then came back here and fell asleep! I must have been more tired than I thought!" She was aware that the proprietor was examining her wrinkled clothes, smeared make-up, and matted hair.

"I see, then you did not have your supper?" She continued her assessment. "Are you hungry?"

"Thirsty, mostly." Risa raised the bottle and glass.

Bertie came around the desk. "You will come with me now and I will make for you something to eat."

Risa started up the stairs. "Oh, no, you certainly don't have to do that. I'm fine, really. I'll have a good breakfast in the morning."

Bertie was having none of it. "No, you come with me. I can see how hungry you are." She waggled a finger in Risa's direction. "Your color is not good."

Risa sighed. There was no getting around this. "Thank you, Mrs. Gian—"

"Bertie."

Risa followed her back into the kitchen, where Bertie pulled a chair out from underneath the wooden dining table, pointing to it for Risa to sit down in, then went about pulling pans from the cupboard and food from the refrigerator.

Risa poured herself a healthy portion of water then sipped.

"You like the pancetta? I have fresh eggs, basil, onion, mushroom. You like the crusty bread?"

Risa almost said, *does the Pope wear white?* but thought

better of it, given where she was. "Yes, it sounds delicious. Thank you, Bertie." She would eat it even if she had to force it down.

Risa asked while watching Bertie work, "Do have a family?"

"Oh, yes. My daughter. She is married. They have two girls. Such mischievous little ones, they are! They live just down the street. My son-in-law comes to the Inn when I must go into town. He does many things here—you know, it is good to have a man around." She added more spices into the pan. "My husband, he passed five years ago. He did everything." She made the signs of the cross with the spatula.

"Oh, I am so sorry to hear."

"Well, he was a good man. You like garlic? How can you not, here in Italy! Everyone likes garlic, right?" She cackled.

Risa smiled. "Who doesn't love garlic."

Bertie flipped the omelet expertly onto a plate, added the crusty bread with a small dish of fresh olive oil, salt, and pepper, then brought the meal to the table. "Here you go! You eat all this up now."

The scent of the food jogged Risa's appetite. She dug in, closed her eyes against the sting of her salivary glands activating. "This is marvelous," she said between bites. And it was.

Bertie sat down with her, dipping a piece of crusty bread in the oil for herself. "I like to cook for my guests. It keeps them coming back to the Inn Firenze."

"I don't blame them! Tell me, how long have you had the Inn?"

"Oh, this goes back to generations, you see. We do many things to make it more modern, but the charm we always keep, do you know what I mean?"

"Yes. You've done a marvelous job."

Bertie chomped on her bread, crumbs falling onto to her ample bosom. "Ay, such a mess I can be."

"You remind me of my Aunt Hildy. You even look a little like her. She is a real mensch, Aunt Hildy is. But you are a *far* better cook."

"What is this, a *mensch*?"

"I'm sorry. It's a Yiddish word for someone who is kind, giving, unselfish."

"Ah!" She nodded, "I like this word mensch. Do you have family, Mrs. Shapiro?"

"Please, call me Risa. I insist."

"Oh, yes, so you told me so earlier. Such a beautiful name. Risa." She rolled her 'r'.

"Thank you. Yes, I have a husband and a daughter. My son," she swallowed before she could continue, "died last year."

Once again, Bertie made the sign of the cross on her chest with a piece of bread. "Oh, I am so very sorry to hear of this news. What a terrible thing. Such a shame. Was he young?"

"Yes. He was." Risa finished her meal in silence. When she was done, she made to stand up with her dishes. "This was so kind of you, really. May I clean up?"

Bertie stood up quickly, scattering crumbs on the floor. She wrapped her knuckles on the wooden table. "Of course not! My guests don't clean up! You see, it was good for you to eat. Your color is better now."

"I feel much better. Thank you so much. I think I will go upstairs, shower, then go back to sleep. Tomorrow is another day."

"It is. If you need anything, Risa, you just come right back down and knock on my door! I sleep sometimes heavy; my husband told me once I snore more than him!" She threw her hands up. "I ask myself, Bertie, how could he know how much I snore when *he* is snoring so loud himself? He would tell me I could wake the dead." She sighed, "But as you can see, he never wakes up."

# CHAPTER THIRTY-SEVEN

*Friday May 7, 1982*
*The Inn Firenze*

A clap of thunder woke her from a sound sleep. The room rumbled and the windows shook in their housing, still open to the rain. Risa jumped out of bed, closed the windows, dried the ledge with a towel from the bathroom, then looked out beyond the Inn. The early morning sky had settled into a gun metal gray from the darkness of the night. Rain was coming straight down, sluicing over sidewalks, the bridge. There would be no lazily drifting pleasure gondolas or market boats making their way down the Arno yet. The streets were quiet. Neon lights from shops cut through the dull light, the bridge still lit from the night before. A taxi streamed by, splashing water around the uneven roadway.

The clock read seven thirty. She was thankful she had slept through the night without any bad dreams. But she was edgy, her insides shaky, the events of yesterday still lingering. And while she appreciated Bertie's concern for her welfare, she had been more embarrassed to be seen in such a shambled state—especially with someone she barely knew.

She sat down on the window ledge, drawing her legs up under her chin, curling her arms around them. She murmured, "It's a gray day, son. Lightning, thunder. Remember how frightened you would get when it thundered? You were only five. We made a game of it. You called it Rabbi's Bowling in Heaven. I thought that was pretty clever of you. Then, as you got older, you and I watched the storms come in from the backyard, daring each other who would run into the house first. You began to think of rain, thunder, and lightning as things of great beauty, a way for mother earth to clear her dark skies. A cleansing. You were so…insightful."

She rested her head on her raised knees and let warm tears drop onto her nightgown. "I'm here. In Italy. Alone. I saw someone yesterday who looked like you. My heart aches again today. I thought maybe I would have a few days of peace, but I guess not."

It was quiet at the Inn. She heard no footsteps or doors closing, or water rushing through pipes. The only ambient sounds filtered in from outside her closed windows, her breaths quietly intermingling.

She looked around the room, taking inventory. The clothes she wore yesterday were in a pile on the chair near the armoire. Items from her big purse were scattered haphazardly on the desk. The towel from her shower of the previous evening hung askew over the top of the bathroom door.

She made a move to get up and take care of the mess, but something kept her where she was. A recent therapy session interrupted her thoughts.

*"What were to happen if you broke from tradition and left your clothes in a pile for a week? Or didn't clean the bathroom after every use, or left your desk unorganized?"*

Risa had answered, "Probably wouldn't happen. When Corey was in the hospital, I certainly left things at home a mess. Dust collecting everywhere! The kitchen was in shambles from Saul and Rachel. The refrigerator had things growing…and don't even ask about the bathrooms!"

*"But did you really, leave things a mess I mean?"*

"No, I guess I didn't. I had a housekeeper come in. Everything was where it was supposed to be when I got home."

She now knew how true that statement was, and at the same time, how utterly sad it was. She continued to survey her belongings in the little room, becoming more disgusted by the moment. She said out loud, "He was dying!"

She realized, with alarming clarity, that everything in her life had been orchestrated by her own hand, a set of rules that kept everything in balance—a so-called normal person's balance. A balance she was convinced was necessary to accomplish her role as a mother to two perfect children and wife to a successful attorney.

If everyone else was happy, she could be happy. Her mother had lovingly called it the Jewish way.

Risa mumbled at the memory. "The Jewish way. What in the hell does that even mean, Mom? What in the hell is the Jewish way?"

*Alice had once said, "Let's try to reset the landscape."*

*To which Risa had answered, "But Corey's lifestyle ruptured that landscape! How do I reset that?"*

She thought, *if Alice was here right now, what would she make of me questioning my motives?*

"Oh, she'd have something to say about it, I'm sure."

Suddenly, her thoughts became edgy.

"And the secrets! I *had* to protect the integrity of the family, and Saul's professional reputation!" She unfolded her legs from underneath her and stood up. "But it was *me* who had to seek the help of a therapist because of the silent deception and betrayal! *I* was forced into it!" Her voice rose. "And what of it? The deception surfaced anyhow! Secrets were revealed and now what?"

She started to pace. "A dead son is what!" The acidity of her words forced her edginess to become more profound, a shrill-like energy crept beneath her shoulders and up through her neck. Her blood pressure rose, and she became lightheaded. Not familiar with this feeling, she stopped pacing in hopes of clearing her head but instead found her hands involuntarily clenched into fists at her sides. Adrenaline coursed through her veins and she began to shake. A wave of nausea spread from her chest into her throat. She fought the desire to vomit. With a few deep breaths, she regained her focus. Her room now became a stage. She assumed a theatrical position directing a monologue to the unmade bed. "The perfect Mrs. Shapiro who couldn't have a normal family! Torn to shreds because of…let the indestructible Mrs. Shapiro take care of it!"

She moved to and fro on her imaginary proscenium, her footfalls heavier with each step. "How could you *do* this to me?" She blurted through clenched teeth. "How could you turn my world upside down and not be here to be accountable for it?"

Then she snapped.

In a blind rage she turned and took two long steps across the room to the armoire, where she wrenched the doors open and yanked clothes off hangers thrashing them behind her. Buttons popped; fabric ripped. "Son. Of. A *bitch!*" She hissed.

She tugged out the drawers; wood clanking to the floor, clothes scattering. She spun and focused her wrath on the desk, where she shoved everything off it in one quick motion with her forearm, glass shattering as it hit the floor. She grabbed the purse from its leather handles and slammed it down on the bed several times.

*"No, no, no!"*

She stood in the middle of the room; her breath coming hard and fast. A brass button from a blazer clung to the arch of her right foot. She stepped on it harder, then stomped and ground her foot on it as it dug into her skin. She grumbled in a low voice, "You go right ahead and take my blood!" Her voice quickly rose to a shrill, *"God knows you've taken everything else!"*

She clawed at the front of her nightgown, feeling a rush of heat, wanting nothing near her skin. She fought with the thin fabric, tearing at it until it slid off her body to the floor.

She turned back to the armoire and stopped short when she saw herself in the mirror; her reflection terrifying her. Her face had morphed into the same bizarre reconfiguration of features she saw on Saul's face the night he learned Corey was gay.

Her hair was wild, unkempt; her body looked foreign. She felt a gust of energy billow from her chest then she quickly raised her fist to her mouth to stifle the on-coming scream. A guttural sound came out forced. "*Aaugh!*" Without warning her knees buckled. She grabbed a clump of clothing and howled into the fabric. Her lungs filled, her heart trip hammered, she could not stop the onslaught of raw emotion curling up and out of her mouth. She pushed the fabric further in to bury the sound.

A rapid knock came at the door. "Mrs. Shapiro! Mrs. Shapiro! It's Mrs. Giancarlo. Bertie!"

Risa's body started to shake. Her head bobbed, her legs twitched, her arms slapped at her sides, and fabric dangled from her mouth. Her muffled screams escalated. She gasped for breath.

A harder, more rapid knock came from the hallway. "Mrs. Shapiro, open this door right now!"

Then, a jangle of keys.

Bertie flung open the door, saw Risa on the floor, quickly entered the room and shut the door behind her, then swiftly knelt to hold her.

## CHAPTER THIRTY-EIGHT

*Inn Firenze*
*The Same Day*
*Noon*

Risa found herself in the bed, covers tucked up around her shoulders. Bertie was sitting in a chair facing her, a concerned look on her face. Risa wondered how long she had been sitting there.

"Risa, do you want me to call someone?"

She shook her head without speaking; her throat was so sore.

Bertie said gently, "I am worried for you."

Riss tried to focus through swollen eyes. "Cold cloth please."

Bertie swayed into the bathroom, ran the cold tap, squeezed out a washcloth then gently wrapped it around Risa's temples. "Here you go, dear."

Risa tried to speak but Bertie shushed her. "We can talk later."

Bertie continued to watch Risa.

Risa pressed the compress down on top of her burning eyes. She felt so sick. Her voice was gravelly. "What happened?"

Bertie sighed. "I think you had a nervous breakdown."

Risa cringed.

Bertie asked quietly, "Are you sure you don't want me to call your husband?"

Risa mumbled, "Yes, I'm sure."

Another few minutes elapsed then Risa said, "I wouldn't blame you if you asked me to leave."

"Why would I ask you to leave?"

Risa grimaced as parts of the episode started coming back to her. "I made a mess of things. I'm sure I disturbed everyone at the Inn."

Bertie moved to sit down on the edge of the bed, her weight

displacing balance. She took Risa's hand in hers. She said in a gentle voice, "Do you know, well, you would not know, how could you? When my Vittorio died, right there in the bed with me right next to him, I screamed like I was getting killed! It took two of my guests to hold me down, one to call the hospital, the other to try to find my daughter and son-in-law. I don't remember much, you see, just that when I came home from the hospital, he was not there. Ever again."

Risa pictured the whole event from behind closed eyes. She had no tears left. "I am so sorry, Bertie," she whispered.

Bertie continued, "You are in great pain, am I right?"

Risa nodded. As if on cue, her right foot throbbed. She vaguely remembered why.

"And Father Paul, he says pain is really our soul crying out. And we must give it its due, do you understand?"

Risa said quietly, "Yes." Then added, "It just came on."

"These things, well, they don't have an exact time."

"No. They don't." Risa took the compress from her eyes and looked at Bertie. "You are a Godsend. A mitzvah."

"A mitzvah? What is this word, another Yiddish again?"

"Yes, it means blessing."

Bertie smiled. "You see? I learned two new words now from the Yiddish. Mensch and mitzvah."

Risa replaced the cloth onto her forehead. She just wanted to sleep.

Bertie patted her hand. "Now. You must rest. I will go downstairs. When you are ready, ring for me." She tilted her head toward the phone on the stand. "I will bring you a tray of food."

"Why are you being so kind to me?"

"Because. You are woman. I am woman. You travel from America to Florence by yourself, without your family. I am so sorry you lost your son."

Risa muffled a grunt.

"Now you listen to Bertie. Today it will be rainy. The boy from the market will deliver fresh food soon. You must eat to get strength. Your tears took your water, Risa, at least that is what Father Paul says. You must drink a lot today." She tapped

the full bottle of San Pellegrino on the table right next to the bed.
    Bertie closed the door behind her.
    The room was awash in gray light.
    Risa stared at the ceiling; she had nothing left.
    She drifted off into a deep sleep.

Letters to Corey

## CHAPTER THIRTY-NINE

*Inn Firenze*
*Later*

Pressure in her abdomen woke her. She opened crust-laden eyes and shifted her head from left to right.

Still in the little room.

Still naked.

She lifted her head slowly.

The rain had stopped, the air now thick with humidity. Slivers of sunlight cast shadows into the corners of the room. Bertie must have opened the windows.

The clock on the night table read three-thirty-nine.

She pushed the covers down, sat up slowly, then felt the pooled sweat between her breasts drip down onto her abdomen and noticed that the sheets were soaked.

"God," she muttered, running her tongue over dry lips.

She swung her legs over the side of the bed, stood up slowly, now understanding what the pressure was, and padded into the bathroom. The tile floor underneath her feet was damp from the humidity. She had to limp; her right foot was achingly sore.

She sat on the commode for a while, deciding what to do next. She barely had the strength to stand up but pushed herself to take a shower. She took her time under the flow of water, washing gently over what felt like sunburnt skin. Her hair felt like a helmet of straw. If she'd had scissors, she would have cut it. She murmured, "Thank God for that…"

She rinsed, turned the temperature down so a cool rainfall of water covered her skin.

A fresh set of towels had been placed in the bathroom while she slept.

She dried off, loath to get back into the sweat laden sheets but knew she needed more sleep, so she calmly stripped the sheets from the bed, putting dry towels down on top of the mattress cover, then positioned herself onto her back.

Sleep came swiftly.

\*\*\*

A quiet but consistent knock came at the door. "Risa?" Bertie's voice floated through the room.

Risa sat up abruptly, the towels a tangled blob underneath her, the pillow still damp from her wet hair. It was dark now.

"Hello?" Risa managed to say, not sure exactly where she was.

"Are you alright? May I come in?"

Risa panicked for a moment. She was still naked, wasn't sure where her clothes were, and had no concept of time. "Can you give me a moment, Bertie?"

"I have some food for you. You must be hungry. Did you drink the water?"

Risa couldn't process all the chatter. She squeezed her eyes shut, took a gulp of air. "Yes. I…" In the dark she stumbled from the bed to the chair next to the armoire and felt around the pile of clothes. She found Saul's old blue Oxford shirt she had packed to keep him close. It smelled like his cologne even though it had been laundered. She wiggled into it, still buttoned. "I'm coming." She tiptoed to the door, opened it and stepped back to let Bertie in.

"I thought you might be hungry. Maybe you want something light, like bread and insalata?"

Risa swallowed. The thought of food was the last thing on her mind. She was thirsty, however, so she reached for the bottle of water and the glass.

Bertie entered the room and set the small tray on the desk. "I thought you would like to eat in your room."

"Thank you. But I—"

"You want maybe I can bring you some pizza and wine? I made a fresh pie this afternoon."

Her taste buds rallied: get sick, or eat? She moved slowly, sipping the water. So far so good. It stayed down. "This is so kind of you."

Bertie noticed the bed. "I will bring fresh sheets."

"I am sorry. I had to pull them off, they were wet from sweat. And the towels." Risa bent over to whisk the towels off the bed when she experienced a wave of dizziness followed by nausea. She sat down awkwardly on the edge of the bed.

Bertie helped her to the desk chair. "You must go slow. You are still without enough water and food."

Risa watched as Bertie removed plate covers. *Doesn't she understand that I'm still woozy?*

Bertie said, "Now, try something like the bread first."

Risa tentatively took a bite of bread; her salivary glands stinging into her ears.

Bertie watched carefully in case Risa faltered.

Risa tried more bread. "It's good."

Bertie smiled. "That's right! Nice and slow. Just a bite or two at a time."

Risa said, as she chewed, "Are you sure you are not Jewish?"

Bertie barked out a laugh. "Jewish, you say? I am Italian! Don't you know Jewish and Italian people are *the same*?" She cackled at her own joke.

Risa shook her head slowly. She'd have to tell this to her mother.

Bertie said, "I will get clean linens while you eat."

Risa's heart and soul felt like a deflated balloon. All she wanted to do was get back into bed.

She eyed the family photograph. A grim recollection of breaking glass filtered through her mind, and she turned away. Bertie must have cleaned up the glass as well. She felt ashamed of herself. Tears developed again, but this time, they were slow to fall, burning her cheeks, pausing on her chin before falling into her lap.

She'd shattered the glass of her family portrait. There was one small shard still held by the frame and its sharp point was positioned stage-right of the family: Rachel and Saul.

She looked away.

*What have I done?*

Bertie gave a quick knock on the door, "It's me again, with your clean sheets and towels. May I come in?"

Risa took another sip of her water. "Of course."

She turned her head back to the photograph and studied it again. All the smiles were there, all the hands touching in the right places.

Corey was seventeen, Rachel had just turned fourteen.

Such a beautiful family.

*So many secrets and lies.*

Bertie expertly snapped the sheets into place and set the towels in the bathroom on the shelves above the commode. She said, from the bathroom, "I want to tell you that your husband called while you were asleep. I told him you caught a little cold, but that you were okay. He seemed concerned. He said you must call him tomorrow." She re-entered the room. "Will you tell him what happened?

Risa shook her head. "No. He'd make me come home, or worse, he would come here. No, I'm on my own with this. Although if it weren't for you…"

"Well, my Vittorio would say things happen for a reason." She put the lids back on the plates and stacked the tray. "I will be downstairs if you need me."

"I just don't know how to thank you—"

Bertie cut her off on her way to the door. "Like I said, things happen for a reason."

After Bertie closed the door behind her, Risa wondered how this perfect stranger, this person from halfway around the world, could be so kind, so loving. Then out of the blue she remembered something—the little pouch in the zippered compartment of her suitcase where she stowed Captain Pegleg and the Black Pearl.

She went to retrieve it.

"How did I forget?" She almost started crying as she sat back down at the desk. "How *could* I forget?" She opened the drawstrings, then gently turned the pouch upside down to catch the trinkets in her palm. She looked at them for a moment then wrapped her fingers around them. With her eyes closed she tried to summon strength from the objects; something, anything to reground her. There was nothing but distant memories.

She put the keepsakes back into the velvet pouch then climbed back into the bed holding the talisman to her heart. At least she could keep something from home close to her.

The clean, crisp cool sheets felt good. She closed her eyes and fell back into another deep slumber.

*\*\*\**

**JOURNAL ENTRY**
*Saturday May 8, 1982*
*Inn Firenze*

*Corey,*
*I had a breakdown yesterday and it all came to the surface—like a volcano. Yes, that is what it was. A volcano. It erupted without control, it frightened me because I could not stop it, it seemed to have no end, and I'm a continent away from the people I love. And if it weren't for Bertie, I don't know how I would have ended up. Probably in a hospital somewhere. I can't even think about it...I'm still scared. Embarrassed. I feel so small and fragile.*

*And I am so hurt. I thought you and I had the most special relationship...but the more I realize how little I knew about you, the more I blame myself for not being the mother you should have had. Do you know how long I've been feeling this way? No, how could you...you were dealing with your own demons that neither your father nor me had any idea about it. You kept it from us, lying to us, insisting that you were happy with Deborah. But you were acting a part in the ultimate play of life. The ultimate deception!*

*Maybe I've been living in some kind of bubble all these years. But why would that be bad? Everyone seemed so happy and satisfied. I was a good provider for you! What did I miss? I gave you all the room you needed to be who you were! Then you went and lied about your deepest emotions, your trueness. Why? I don't understand! Why?*

*I feel like I'm getting myself all worked up again. Maybe I should go back to bed. Yes, I think I will do that. I will go back to bed.*
*Love,*

*Mom*

She slept for another five hours.

***

Later that day, Bertie sat with her while she had some lunch. "Your color is looking better today, Risa. It's good to see you eat. You like the pizza?"

Risa nodded. "I'm sorry I don't come downstairs to eat, Bertie."

Bertie lifted her chin while still watching her. "You don't have to do anything you don't want to. Bertie will take care of things. My daughter is here today, getting ready for the new guests who will arrive soon."

Risa panicked. "Did you tell her there is a crazy woman on the second floor?"

Bertie shrugged and chuckled, "Well, I said you weren't feeling well and that I would tend to you myself. You are not crazy woman."

"You are a wonderful mother, Bertie. May I ask you a question?"

"Of course, you can ask as many questions as you like."

"Do you think you know your daughter well?"

"Well? Do I think I know…" she looked off for a moment, then said, "I think so I do. She is a lot like me, of course. A little less big in the bosom, her hair is still brown."

"Of course. But do you know *who* she is?"

"You mean like in the heart?" She tapped her chest with three fingers. "She is like my Vittorio. Strong in heart. She loves her daughters like I loved her when she was young."

"I have no doubt. But, what if your daughter is something you weren't aware of but thought you knew her through and through?"

Bertie wrinkled her brows. "I don't think I understand, Risa. What are you saying?"

"I thought I knew my son. We were so close. We did everything together. While he was growing up, I took him everywhere with me, taught him everything I could about the outside world. And then, I realized before he died that maybe I did not know him at all—that I had been living in some kind of dream world or something."

Bertie asked, "That *you* lived in the dream world or *him* in the dream world?"

Risa cocked her head and thought about it for a moment. "Hm. You make an interesting point."

"I think, maybe, Risa, that children keep secrets all the time. Don't we all?"

"I am an open book with my husband, my kids, my family…I didn't have to keep secrets until I found out my son had been lying to me for months. Maybe even years."

"Lying? What would he lie about for so long?"

Risa thought about what she would say. Should she divulge the ugly truth? Would Bertie see her in a different, darker light? "He was *gay*, Bertie."

Bertie nodded and raised her eyebrows. "My sister's son, Arturo, he is also a gay man. He now lives in Rome. My sister did not like it at all, she kicked him out of the house. Me? I don't really care one way or the other. I see every kind of person here at the Inn. Now, Vittorio, he did not like the gays at all. But I say, 'Vittorio! Money is money!' and he would say, 'Not under my roof!' and I tell him to be quiet!"

Risa repositioned herself in the bed. "He died of HIV."

Bertie made the signs of the cross. "Oh, poor boy. I hear terrible things about this HIV. I am so sorry. It must have been very awful for you and your family."

"It was. It still is," she said emphatically.

The women sat with each other in companionable silence until Bertie stood up, straightened the sheets, and put her hand on top of Risa's. "Now, you listen to Bertie. Maybe today you will come downstairs and join us for a glass of wine?"

"I don't know. I look a fright. My hair… maybe soon you can recommend a hair salon? I want to cut it all off. It's too thick and heavy. Maybe sometime next week? And my nails." She looked down at her fingers. "Ugh."

Bertie nodded, "I know just the place! I will make the

appointments for you. You tell me when you want to go."

"Thank you. I will."

After Bertie left the room, Risa eyed the pile of clothes on the chair. They looked like someone else's. She wasn't even sure who she was now; feeling caught between two worlds, an unfamiliar limbo. She got out of bed and stepped over to the desk chair.

***

## JOURNAL ENTRY

*Every time I look at this photograph I shudder. How could I break the very glass that held us all together? I'm so sad about this.*

*Right now, today, feels like a chasm between what I was when I arrived here a few days ago and now. I can't even look in the mirror—I know what I look like without it. I've lost something—and it's not only my son. I've lost something of me. Maybe it's been lost all along? I always had a visible plan, a path to a goal. Rachel's words continue to haunt me—have I been that blind? Is this normal? Do all us mothers think we are doing the right thing for our children only to find out we got tripped up along the way without our knowledge, speeding right along like an uninformed idiot? That's what I feel like right now! An idiot! Blind! How did I miss all the signs? Alice says I wasn't looking for them, so how would I know? But I <u>SHOULD HAVE KNOWN</u>!*

She was getting riled up again, so she dropped the pen next to the journal, crawled back into bed, and went to sleep.

## CHAPTER FORTY

*Inn Firenze*

The phone chirped twice. Risa reached over and picked up the receiver. "Hello?"

The overseas operator said, "I have a person-to-person call from Saul Shapiro for Risa Shapiro, do you accept?"

"I do."

"Go ahead, sir."

"Risa?!"

"Hi honey." The room was dark. She checked the clock on the nightstand. It was eight o'clock.

"What is going on over there? The proprietor said you were sick with a cold!"

"I was. I'm feeling much better now. I'm sorry I didn't call. I've been sleeping, mostly."

"Are you eating?"

"I am. How could one turn down the incredible food here?" she chuckled.

This seemed to mollify him. In a calmer voice, he said, "I was pretty worried about you. I almost got on a plane."

"No need. Believe it or not Mrs. Giancarlo, she likes to be called Bertie, has been taking expert care of me."

"Well, that worked out well. I'm glad she is there."

Risa thought the same. "What have you been up to?"

"Work, of course. The house. Rachel and I are going to drive to New York City tomorrow to get Corey's belongings. It's time."

Risa took a deep breath; secretly glad she was not there to make the trip. "Okay. Please let Rachel drive one of the ways?"

"Of course. She's a great highway driver."

"Thank you for doing this, Saul. I know I should be there, but…"

"But nothing. I'll put his stuff in the basement. We can go through it at a later date."

"Thank you."

"Well, I just wanted to hear your voice, make sure you were okay, and that I didn't need to get on the next plane. I miss you. *We* miss you."

"I miss you, too. Give Rachel and hug and kiss for me. It'll be better received coming from you, anyhow."

"Now Reese, let's not go there. She's a pretty resilient young lady and I think she's remorseful about what she said. She's a typical teenager."

"And under strenuous circumstances. No teenager should have to go through what she went through."

Saul said quietly, "*No* one should have to go through what we went through."

Risa agreed silently. "I'll call you soon, honey. Don't worry about me, I'm going to be just fine."

After ending the call, she got up, stretched, and went to the window ledge. The night was full of neon lights. People talking, laughing, going somewhere, living.

Living.

Risa sat down at the desk and turned on the little lamp.

\*\*\*

## JOURNAL ENTRY

*Hello son.*

*Living. That's what people do. They live. They laugh, cry, love, eat, sleep, think, do. They live. But what happens when life breaks life itself? Blood still pumps through my body and things get fed, but how do I start living again? Where is the spark? How will I know where to find the spark? What would Alice say? She would say something pragmatic, of course. Something so simple that...she might say it has to come from within. But how does it* <u>get there</u>, *within? Is it buried somewhere? I don't know. Right now, I look at what I brought with me to Italy, and I think, these things belong to someone else.*

*It will be Sunday in another few hours. The day of rest. People will have fun tonight, go out, drink, dance, share in laughter and conversation. They will stay up late because they won't have to wake up early to go to work.*

I remember those nights, in Cambridge, when your dad and I were first married. We had such a fun social life. Movies, plays, concerts, trips up to Maine to the Lobster Pot. Saul's Corvette convertible. Flying through the marsh lands, the countryside, and the sea to our right on the way up, to the left on the way home. So carefree. Full of great conversations and laughs.

But then your dad was busy at Grandpa Nate's law firm, working his way up the ladder. I was doing small community plays, mostly comedies, and loving every moment of it. I lived for the camaraderie of the actors—in our short run time we would become a family. And when the run was over, it would be a sad day...but then, another play, another chance to be a family again. We became this little elite group—Saul used to call it a secret society. We were. We knew who was directing what, who was a shoe-in. How to audition. The motion was constant.

And then when you came along, we were already in Manchester and my life took a completely different path. I became pregnant shortly after our move and while I was excited to start a family, I admit I had regrets. No more crazy Cambridge nights, no more daily rehearsals and shows. No more leaving town on a weekend whim, or a moveable feast party with our neighborhood friends.

Manchester was a big step into the country club elite. I had to dress more conservatively, look and act the part of the successful housewife. And luckily I'm a good actress and believe you me, there were times I had to pour it on because the ladies of Cape Ann could be so snobby, and uptight!

So, I got involved with the Jewish Community Center in the theatre department and it was good—not as crazy or bohemian as Cambridge—but the scripts were solid. A couple of us gals started a little comedy troupe called The Capers. We wrote our own plays and performed for fund-raising events. We even got written up in the Cape Ann Examiner, people came to events just to see us lampoon! We did a few official roasts. Those were the most fun. But you know all of this—if you even remember it...

But then, Corey, I had you. And as you know, the first four

*months were so difficult, I was lost but then one night I found my journey with your being. Oh, honey, I couldn't wait to bundle you up, get you in the stroller, and walk for what seemed like miles—just showing you all that nature had to offer. We went all year round. And when you weren't sleeping, you were entranced with the life around you. You pointed at everything, had interesting words for things before you knew what they were. We would stop and look at pinecones, acorns, leaves. Of course, you tried to eat all these things, too! You loved the birds, squirrels, chipmunks, horses, cats, dogs...oh you squealed with delight! I loved how you looked at life—it taught me that the simple things were what truly mattered. But then, the simple things seemed to get lost in the shuffle of raising two children. There was always something to be done.*

*As you grew older, I took you into Boston on the train. Oh, honey, you loved the train! I'd hold onto your chubby little legs as you stood at the window and watched the landscape zip by. You'd make train noises when it stopped in the station. You were like a sponge. Nothing scared you, Core. The more I exposed you to, the more you wanted. Nothing could hold you back! So, we went, we went, and we went—everywhere. I loved it.*

*And watching you grow—it was an experience that filled me up daily. Your sense of wonder, that pure unadulterated wonder.*

Risa stopped to relieve the cramp in her hand and drink some water. She couldn't get the words out fast enough.

*You and Rachel loved watching the old black and white movies with me when dad had to stay in Boston overnight for work. You knew all the big players by heart. You thought Cary Grant was very handsome. Should I have known then? But you also liked Joan Crawford and Myrna Loy. I should have known then...*

*You and Rachel...the most precious pieces of me and your dad...*

*And I know your dad wasn't always available for us, but he was busy at work, making the money so we could live a perfect*

*life.*
*And I was busy making it perfect for us.*

Risa reread the last line. Perfect life. She thought about it for a moment then continued.

*Was it perfect? Your dad was a good provider. We had the comforts of home. We took such fun trips together...I loved the goofy car rides the best. Remember we'd play I Spy? You and Rachel, dad and I...what a foursome.*

*Then you two started growing into yourselves. Rachel became the pragmatic miniature version of her father, you kept wondering about the world, but I could tell, something was a little different about you. Were you unsettled? A restless soul? I keep looking back, finding a time when I should have noticed.*

*I must keep remembering Alice's words: 'You didn't know to look for it, so how would you know?' She's right. But then again, I remember talking with Peg over one of our many lunch dates. I told her there was something special about you, but I couldn't put my finger on it. She said you were years ahead of your handsomeness. That the girls would be knocking on our door. Little did I know that the boys would be knocking, too.*

*So, I am beginning to understand your unsettledness. Maybe I've been unsettled, too? I lived my life as I saw fit, but there were times I just wanted to stop—stop everything and sit for a while. Sit and re-assess. Reassess what, though? As I look back and think how everyone saw me as the stronghold of the family, the working actress, the busy mom, the one who cleaned up when we were all sick, the one who packed suitcases, made the arrangements, kept the timetable well oiled. Cooked, chauffeured...the list is too long.*

*And all for what? You're gone. And I keep getting tangled up in all the reasons, the possibilities, the what ifs.*
*You're gone. Period.*

Risa stopped writing. She got up from the chair and stretched her limbs then went back to the ledge at the window. "So many questions that will never have an answer. How do I live with that?"

She used the bathroom, looked in the mirror, and shook her head. "God, what a mess."

She paced the little room, trying to keep her footfalls light. A part of her wanted to go downstairs and see if there was any left-over pizza in the fridge. But another part of her did not want to engage Bertie in conversation. She was more than grateful for Bertie's intervention but needed things to be quiet.

She sat back down on the bed. Decided it was too much of a hassle to put on clothes and make herself presentable.

She added a PS to the journal entry.

*Wouldn't it be nice if I could remove my heart from my chest, set it in some calming waters for a while, then when I'm ready, put it back into my body so I can breathe again? Wouldn't that be so much better instead of all the wear and tear we impose on it?*

\*\*\*

## JOURNAL ENTRY
***Sunday May 9, 1982***
***Early Morning***

*I had a dream last night. It was your funeral. There were many people there I did not recognize. People who wanted to wish us condolences. It was Rabbi Rothman presiding. Your father and sister stood next to me while my mother and father and the rest of our family and friends stood behind us. Michael was there, looking so handsome and strong even though I knew he was crumbling inside. We took up an entire section. There was music, not sure where it was coming from, but it was just beautiful. Bittersweet. Sad and uplifting at the same time. And there you were, your picture above your casket—closed. There was no way to make you look like you did before you became ill. And the flowers. All along the pulpit, magnificent colors. Colors that spoke of who you were in your short life. Peg made the floral arrangements.*

Unwilling to stop long enough to get a tissue, she wrote around tears that dropped onto the page. She would not dab them away. She would let them soak in the paper so they would always be there.

*And then, at the graveside, just the family. And Michael. I wanted him there. He deserved to be there. He loved you. Thank God for Michael in your short life. I held his arm the entire time.*
*Maybe this was not a dream, dear Corey, but a recollection. Yes, this is how it happened. I've blocked it out until just now.*
*The days afterward are a blur. All I remember was coming home and walking aimlessly around the house. Then the days blended with semi-awareness...of going on with the business of running the household. Grandma Ruthie was there for weeks, I think.*
*Your father. He was stricken. I'd find him at his desk, just sitting there facing the window to the back yard. I would go to him, pull up a chair, and sit. No words, no tears. Just our own thoughts. He would reach for my hand and squeeze it three times. It meant; I love you. It was our secret handshake before we got married.*
*We hadn't done that in a long time, son. We seem to have substituted other things for that handhold...*
*We continue to live through the loss of a child.*

She stopped writing, re-read what she wrote, then changed gears.

*I used to listen to my dad play his viola in the living room when I was younger. I would get on the couch and arrange the pillows around my head so I couldn't see any light. The music would carry me off and away; the magnificence of the notes lulling me into a trance-like state. You know, for such a big guy with a stogie sticking out of his mouth most of the time, he played that instrument like it was an extension of his soul, closing his eyes and disappearing into the complexity of the music written by masters. And he made it look so easy. And when other musicians came over to the house to rehearse, it was a gift. These men, in their undershirts and trousers with suspenders hanging off their arms! My God, they made those instruments sing! I loved my father for his deep respect for the music he played and exposed me to.*

*He loved you, Corey, like he loved his music. And when I finally had to tell them about you, he didn't flinch for a moment!*

*He knew how much you loved the music of Aaron Copland, So, it was just a few months ago that your father and I attended a BSO concert. While the orchestra was tuning up, Grandpa Abe approached the microphone and said, 'I would like to dedicate this evening's performance to my grandson, Corey Joseph Shapiro, who lost his life in October of last year from HIV.'*

*The audience, the orchestra, all went silent. Then came clapping, then a standing ovation. Your father and I were stunned and moved at the same time. We both had tears in our eyes as we stood and applauded. It was a night of Copland's music, a night we shall never forget.*

*Bertie Giancarlo is another angel in our midst. She has taken care of me for three straight days—three straight days that I haven't left the room. She makes sure I am fed, watered, and laundered (if you will). It's nice having someone who tends to my needs for once. For me to give in and let a perfect stranger nurse me. I had no choice but to surrender to her. I couldn't very well call Alice, and your father would probably insist I come home immediately—he did threaten to get on a plane when he didn't hear from me for a few days.*

*I'm ready to change me, Corey. I'm going to start with my hair, then my nails, then my clothes. I need to lighten the load. To get with the times, like you used to say. Maybe the outside changes will help heal the inside. I'm beginning to understand what Alice is talking about—about how grief can last a lifetime, the only thing that really changes is how well one can weave it into their routine. She said, 'You never forget, you just learn to accept it.' Because, really, we have no choice, do we?*

*I think I might be able to venture out tomorrow. Here I am in this glorious city of history, and I am landlocked in this little room. But like Bertie says, things happen at exactly the time they are supposed to happen. She has a lot of insight, Bertie does.*

*I recall a beautiful sermon by Rabbi Kushner—about how we are connected by pieces of a jigsaw puzzle; that we hold certain pieces and when we meet someone, it isn't coincidence; it is more about that we supply those pieces for another person and vice-versa. I suppose I could say meeting you was—no, no...that doesn't apply. Or does it?*

*So, son. I am going to take the rest of the day to go through my belongings, pull myself together and go downstairs for a meal or two. Maybe even a glass of wine!*

*I will write again soon,*
*I miss you.*
*Your loving mom*

She sat stock still, the journal still open to the pages she wrote. For a moment, she panicked. The writing offered her a safe place where she could spend uninterrupted time with her heart, with Corey, without looking at a clock; pouring everything out from random thoughts to embedded feelings. "I won't stop," she promised herself. "It's keeping me sane. Or as sane as I could be right now."

She capped her pen and laid it in the crevice between the pages of the book and listened to the ambient sounds around her: footfalls and doors closing, floors creaking in the hallways, Bertie's husky Italian sotto voiced conversations with the new guests from the lobby two flights down the stairs, someone laughing, quiet exchanges of voices passing by. Cars and motorbikes zoomed below her opened windows, boats on the Arno slid through the calm waters. It was Sunday in Florence. Tourists would flock to the Piazza's; street vendors would hawk their wares; stores would have their front doors open to the fresh summer air. Olive oil would be pressed and sold.

She took one more look at the family photo, felt her heart lurch quickly then recover, and stood up.

It was time to start living; one step at a time.

# Letters to Corey

## CHAPTER FORTY-ONE

*Florence, Italy*
*Friday May 15, 1982*

Risa entered a small pizzeria. She was pleasantly exhausted, having finished her two-and-a-half-day tour of the Medici Palace, Chapels, and Duomo Museum.

With her salad, pie-for-one, and juice-glass sized red table wine, she sat at a small table which faced the street, eating slowly, savoring each bite and sip of wine. Her thoughts ambled from the sights she had just seen to how comfortable she felt with the pace of the historic city.

She had made good on her promise to take care of herself. She cut her hair stylishly short—the hairdresser said the sassy look was all the rave—and bought a whole new set of clothes—having donated most of what she brought with her to Bertie's church.

From head to toe, she fit in.

Bertie assured her, "You will be mistaken for Italian!"

To which Risa had replied, "I don't mind that at all. Italian women are stunning. It's a compliment."

She was thinking of taking the train to the wine country on Monday. Bertie had friends who owned a small Inn there and would gladly make the arrangements when Risa was ready.

She had written in her journal the night before, highlighting the sights of her excursions, realizing that she had written very little about her emotional state.

She re-read something Alice had copied for her, pulling it from a clip at the back of her journal.

*"... and while anger, denial, and hurt are still prevalent, the passage to surrender will be tenuous at best, like a bridge without a lot of support. You are familiar with grief and, if you will, the thought of letting it go could mean letting go of something seemingly safe. As much as happiness and peace can*

*be a safe place, so can hurt and denial. But what is better? Getting through it, of course! Why? Because circumventing it just means you will circle back to it. Going through it means you've done the hard work and can move forward. Your grief will, as we've spoken about before, be constant. It is how you manifest the pain into your daily life that will see the most change. Let yourself feel. Let the walls come down brick by brick..."*

After reading the passage in Alice's office that day, she remembers how reluctant she was to let go of her pain. To her, it meant letting go of Corey, and she was not ready for that. Alice had to remind her that *letting go* of pain, and pain, was not one and the same. That her closeness to Corey was not—even though it was easiest to revert to during times of grief—anchored by pain alone.

But now, today, in the small café so far from home, she was beginning to understand the process that Alice was talking about. That she did not have to associate pain with Corey.

***

Later that evening, Bertie invited Risa to the kitchen to help her prepare the weekend meals for guests. They worked together, side by side, as if they had been doing this for years.

"Bertie, can I ask you something?"

"Of course, Risa. Give me that garlic clove, please?"

Risa reached over and grabbed the clove. Handing it to her, she said, "My daughter Rachel..."

"Yes, your daughter Rachel." She chopped it like a machine—the garlic minced in seconds.

"She hates me. We are barely speaking. I was hoping this summer we could repair whatever damage has been done before she goes off to college."

Bertie cupped the minced garlic and tossed it into a big pot, steaming it with homemade red sauce, pancetta, kalamata olives, capers, and bristly sardines. "She does not hate you. Daughters think they do, but they don't. Why would you think that?"

Risa chopped fresh romaine, cucumbers, and fennel. "I don't think I've been very present in her life. She's always been closer to Saul. They are like two peas in a pod. And when Corey went off to college, we started to bond a little more. She was so busy at school and the country club. She was on every team possible, took sailing and tennis lessons...and I was very involved in the theatre."

"Oh? You act on the stage?"

"Yes, on the community level. I never had enough time with the kids growing up to qualify for equity on bigger stages."

Bertie smiled and waggled her kitchen knife in Risa's direction, "I thought maybe you were something more than just a regular housewife. You have that looks."

Risa smiled, "Yes, I've been told that before." She picked up a bunch of fresh basil and rinsed it. While shaking it out and setting it on a towel, she said, "When Corey became ill, all bets were off, do you know what I mean? I closed myself off, I lived for Corey's health. Saul, Rachel, my parents and family, my best friend—who I might add was the angel in my pocket—"

Bertie nodded, "Every woman needs an angel in her pocket, or pocketbook!" She cackled at her own joke. "Go on."

"I just lost focus on everything."

"Your son was dying," she said matter-of-factly. "It stands to reason. You're a mother, he was your child."

Risa felt the sadness collect in her chest. She stopped what she was doing and looked up toward the ceiling, allowing a few tears to develop and drop. She dried her eyes with the towel over her shoulder. "You know, I just want things to go back to normal. But then again, I'm not even sure what normal is." She looked at Bertie now. "Do you know what I mean?"

Bertie shrugged, "Well, of course you are being here in Florence today is not your regular place to be, but I think maybe you will go home a different person?"

Risa nodded. "Well, for one thing, my hair has never been this short, my clothes are different. Saul is either going to love the transformation or raise his eyebrows and nod politely. But really, whose life is it anyhow?"

"It is yours, Risa Shapiro."

"My therapist would love you, Bertie."

"What, you talk to a doctor?"

"I do. She got me through the whole ordeal with Corey. If it weren't for her, I don't know what I'd be doing today."

Bertie lowered her voice. "My daughter and son-in-law thought after Vittorio died I should speak with the doctor. But I speak with my priest. And he helped me so." She made the sign of the cross on her chest. "But, back to your Rachel. I think maybe you will take her on a little trip before she goes to university. Maybe just mother and daughter?"

"I was thinking of that, Bertie. Maybe I'll take her up to Maine for a girl's weekend. Lobsters, crab legs, bike riding along the sea, walks, shopping."

"Oh, to see Maine. I hear such things about how beautiful it is."

"Have you ever been to America, Bertie?"

"I went to New York once to see family but, the Inn is so busy and now with Vittorio gone…"

Risa almost asked her to come to Massachusetts, but something stopped her midway through. "I understand."

They worked again in silence, chopping, stirring, washing, drying. Before Risa went up to her room, she said, "Thank you again for making the arrangements in Tuscany."

Bertie said, "It's what we do here, at Inn Firenze. We take care of our guests."

Risa took off her apron and smoothed out her capri slacks. "Yes, you do. You go above and beyond. And I will suggest the Inn to anyone I know who might be traveling here in the future." She was also going to say something about bringing Saul back, but again something stopped her midway through. "I'm going to go up and take a nap then change for dinner. Everything smells divine!"

***

Before Risa fell off to sleep that night, she sighed deeply. She so enjoyed talking with Bertie. She had written in her journal how it was so much easier to talk with a stranger because they needed to know only certain truths; that the whole story needn't be told.

Rabbi Kushner's pieces of the puzzle.

She slept peacefully.

# Letters to Corey

## CHAPTER FORTY-TWO

*Tuscany, Montepulciano, Italy*
*Mueble il Riccio Inn*
*Monday May 18, 1982*

After a stunning train ride through rolling hills and small towns, Risa finally made it to the Inn. While it had charm, it was larger than Bertie's place and more populated. But her room, on the top floor, had magnificent views across the Tuscan valley. It was run by Gio and Ivana Riccio and their son Iocopo. They were genuinely lovely people, humble and willing to go the extra mile for their guests. Iocopo offered personalized tours of the area.

Risa stood at the open window and drank in the panoramic view of the countryside. "God," she said. "Where else on earth?"

The scent of early summer filled the room. Clean, clear, no noise pollution, no boats, no taxis, or motor scooters. Just the rhythmic sway of tall grasses. She went about unpacking her new, smaller bag. Most of her clothes now were travel worthy and easy to clean. She bought a new pair of walking shoes to replace the four useless ones she brought with her: the soft Italian leather already conforming to her feet.

Once settled, she called Bertie, as promised, to tell her she had arrived safely. Then she called Saul. Then she stowed her journal and pen in her smaller purse and went in search of a café. She was pleasantly hungry.

\*\*\*

**JOURNAL ENTRY**

*Hello son,*
*Here I am in Tuscany. It feels so far away from everything I know. These people live in these small towns on the edge of the*

*countryside. What it must have been like so many years ago, before throngs of people descended upon their humble towns...the cobblestone streets and stone buildings, set so close as if they are leaning on one another—God forbid an earthquake! Their way of life...is it so different from ours? We work, we play, we take care of our family. But here, we should be honored to spend a little time with their way of life—it seems less bustling, less hectic, less fraught with aggression and politics. And the history. We have a lot of history in America, sure. But here, it seems more intricate.*

*Remember the time we took the historic tour of New York City? You were fourteen. Rachel and your dad decided to go to the Natural History Museum. You and I wanted to hear about all the different ethnic neighborhoods.*

*Our two favorites—of course—were the Italian and Jewish sections. All the delicatessens! How many on one block alone? You loved the hustle and bustle, I loved the closeness of the buildings, the stores, the shop windows. I never knew that the original delicatessens were of German Jew descent!*

*Bertie and I talked about reincarnation the other night. I've always been one to believe that we live, we die, and that's it. She thinks we will come back after we die. The more wine I drank the more I was open to the idea. She says the soul leaves the body upon death. Where does it go? She asked. Out into the universe, I guess. She says she believes the soul comes back to where it found love. She tells me about visits from a ghost she thinks is Vittorio. She says he comes to her at the most different of moments. But sometimes she can smell his aftershave!*

*Then I wondered about you. Are you here with me? Were you sending a message when I saw your double at the café last week? Well, all it managed to do was cause me to have a complete breakdown. Maybe that was the purpose of seeing him at that precise moment? But, if what Bertie says can be true— that the soul comes back to where it found love—then, it would stand to reason that you are here, right here, with me now.*

She stopped writing to reread what she had written. Maybe it was true, that the soul revisited the place of strongest love.

And then she had an uncomfortable thought, what if Corey's true love was not her but with Michael?

She finished her meal in deep thought. The accusation Rachel had made about how her love for Corey appeared deeper than her love for her husband had gotten stuck in the back of her mind. Was her love for her son unusual? Unhealthy? Unbelievable? Perhaps.

For a moment, she felt naked, exposed by her own realization. She quickly pushed her plate away and picked up her pen again.

*Have I been living in some kind of dream world all my life? Did my family see my dedication to you as something deeper than it should have been? What exactly did I feel that night so many years ago when you were four months old? I thought it was a mother's intense love for her first offspring. Was it odd that I never felt that way with Rachel? Would some people think I was in love with you? Oh God, No! It was a mother's love! I am in love with your father, he is my soulmate! It's a completely different kind of love! You were our offspring, the physical result of our love!*

She needed to take a break from deep thinking, it had the potential to upset her again, so she watched the people around her. There were several different nationalities, touring just like her. Then she noticed an older man sitting at a table by himself watching her. He had a shock of white hair, which framed a deeply wrinkled tanned face. He was dressed in a light brown caftan of sorts, his arms, legs, and hands spindly.

He raised his wine glass to her, nodded, then sipped while still watching her. She returned the gesture. He continued to watch her. At first, she felt uncomfortable. She wondered what was captivating this man so.

The waiter approached her table and cleared her plates. "How do you like today?"

"It was marvelous, molto bene!"

The waiter smiled broadly, "Ah, grazie Signora! Our panna cotta is delicious, would you like to try?"

She nodded, "Of course!"

The elderly man finished his wine, stood up, and walked toward her table. He had something in his hand resembling postcards. She watched in curiosity as he set one of the cards down on her table.

She said, "What is this?"

He tapped the card with a yellowed fingernail and said in a gentle, quiet voice, "This is what you need today."

She watched him walk away, then picked up the cream-colored card with magenta-colored writing on it.

In beautiful flowing script, it said:

*If light is in your heart, you will find your way home.*

## CHAPTER FORTY-THREE

*Wednesday, May 20*
*Tuscany*

**JOURNAL ENTRY**

*Dearest Corey,*
*After two days of touring the backcountry with Iocopo, I am pleasantly peaceful and fulfilled. He is a lovely man, married to Katania—she is from Barcelona—who prepared a meal the likes I have not had, maybe ever. The fish was so fresh—just caught in the morning—and the vegetables were from her tiered garden out back of their home. Of course, the wine parings were second to none! And the bread and olive oil. All I can say is 'oy'!*

*Iocopo brought me to a lovely area of town for shopping. I ambled along the cobblestoned streets, taking in the diverse architecture and open-doored shops along the way. I stopped at a leather smith and found a gorgeous frame for Alice's daughter's photograph. It was hand stitched with flowers on the four corners. The leather is soft and lush. The maker signed the back of the frame! I also found another journal—would you believe I've filled most of this one? The one Alice gave me? The new journal has fine paper and smells divine. Oh, and I found a beautiful guest register for Bertie. Hers is quite worn and falling apart. It is the least I can do for all her ministrations. Bertie...*

*I stumbled upon an amphitheater in the center of town. People sat on the surrounding stone ledges with little coolers of wine and appetizers. The actors on the stage—of course all spoke Italian and I had no idea what they were saying—were very entertaining. The audience laughed heartily, and the action indicated it must have been a farce. I found myself laughing with everyone else—especially when some of the slapstick shticks occurred.*

*You know, son, I realized then, at this town theatre with the sun setting high on the Tuscan countryside in this little slice of* heaven, how much I miss the stage. I wish you could have experienced this with me, us.

The men, I will say, are just so handsome. If I were younger and not married to your father—who I adore and love to the ends of the earth—I'd be...what? I am laughing right now...laughing! And don't think for a moment your old ma hasn't been whistled and stared at! You'd like my new look. It's clean, simple, and my clothes fit. I love my hair, it's so easy to manage—no more thick tangles to comb out. Just towel dry, fluff, and let it wave! And I'm wearing just enough make-up to accentuate my features. My face feels lighter!

But alas, I digress. It is dark outside, just a few lights blinking below. I can imagine the expanse of the vineyards outside my window. Such a life to live...but I must go home eventually. Another week and I'll be flying west. Home...I feel like it's on another planet. A part of me is ready to go, another part is frightened of slipping back into the darkness.

Rachel. I must come to terms with your sister. She is cordial, pleasant just enough to get by. But the tension before I left for Italy was palpable. I'm thinking of taking her up to Maine for a weekend, just the two of us, maybe we can bridge the gap.

And I'm ready to get back to Alice, too. I have so much to share with her. I'll probably see her long enough to put one of her sons through college! Oh...I am so very grateful for her. She was, is(?) my beacon to sanity. Without her...well, I don't even want to imagine that...

I'm heading back to Florence tomorrow afternoon. To my safe, sweet room at the Inn Firenze. To Bertie. I can't wait to tell her about my excursions...I've got a few trinkets for Dad and your grandparents. I found this beautiful wooden replica of a violin; carved, with strings and tuning pegs, for Grandpa Abe, and a miniature hand-blown glass sewing machine for Grandma Ruthie. I bought a beautiful pair of gloves for your father, and a stylish leather jacket for Rachel. Since I have all this extra room in my suitcase now...oh, and a leather vest for Peg.

Okay. I'm bushed. Pleasantly bushed.

I miss you so...

Your loving mom

## CHAPTER FORTY-FOUR

*Inn Firenze*
*Tuesday May 26, 1982*

Bertie poured another glass of wine for herself. "Would you like more?" she asked Risa.

"I'd better not. I have to pack."

"Well, I'm so glad you are feeling better. You look like a different person now."

"I've changed my look."

"No, it's not that. I think it is about your whole body, do you see what I am saying?"

"Yes, I do." Risa sighed, swirling the last of her wine in her glass while looking off beyond the terrace behind the Inn. "I feel different, for sure. But I must admit, Bertie, I'm a little nervous about going home. This has been such a life-changing journey. A part of me wishes I could just stay here and make new memories."

"Of course, I understand that. And think of all the memories you already *will* take home with you!"

The women were silent for a while then Bertie said, "I hope you will make good with your daughter. She is still young."

Risa murmured, "Yes, I plan on it. The more I think about it, the more I realize that I've taken her for granted. She is strong and smart. I always knew she could land on her feet regardless of the situation. But I don't think I gave her enough compassion while Corey was sick, then…died."

Bertie nodded while she sipped her wine. "I think maybe it is always that way. When Vittorio died, I went, how do you say, into myself?"

"Yes, I understand that."

"I went into myself. I felt that I had to continue with the Inn. It was every day, every minute of the day. And at night, for so long of time, I cried myself to sleep."

Risa reached out her hand and set it on Bertie's arm. "You

are such a brave woman, Bertie." She gave her arm a squeeze then released her hold. "Do you believe people meet for a reason?"

"I think it is that way, yes."

"So, we were supposed to meet, don't you think?"

Bertie set her wine glass down. "I think, Risa, everything was just right for us to meet. I could tell that day almost three weeks ago, when you came into the Inn, you were going to be a special guest."

Risa chuckled, "A guest special indeed." She looked at Bertie then laughed, "Little did you know!"

Bertie laughed too. "Oh, my dear. When God puts two people together, for whatever reason, it is…oh, what is the word I look for…serendipita."

"Yes, serendipity. Perfect word. You know, there is a Rabbi back home who wrote a beautiful poem about how we are all unfinished puzzles when we are born. And that people enter our lives to bring the right piece, and vice versa. And" she added with a touch of sadness because she knew in the bottom of her heart that it was going to be true, "sometimes those people move on, and we never see them again. That their purpose has been fulfilled."

Bertie looked at Risa and nodded her head. "I think that is also true. I feel that way between you and I, Risa. Maybe you'll come back to Florence someday and stay at the Inn Firenze, maybe you won't."

"And maybe you will come to America."

Both women knew this would not happen.

Risa took a deep breath and stood up. "Well, my dear friend, I must go upstairs and pack. My flight is at nine-fifty."

"Yes. And again, thank you for the beautiful guest book. It will always remind me of you."

Risa felt her throat close as she entered the Inn, set her wine glass down near the kitchen sink, all so familiar now, and made her way up the stairs to her room.

***

## JOURNAL ENTRY

*The pull to stay here is stronger than I thought. When I pack, I will leave the old skin behind. I will have several hours of flying time to reacclimate my focus. But for now, I just want to sit still, in this lovely room with the slanted floor, the old armoire, the desk laden with nicks and scratches, the slightly canted window ledges, the thin curtains that billow with the night breezes off the Arno.*

*In Tuscany, I felt…alive. Maybe more so than ever. It's hard to say. I remember Peg and I talked about past lives once when we were tipsy at her house. We joked around that we were old movie stars a la Gloria Swanson and Myrna Loy. But maybe there is some truth to that. Oh, not that we were reincarnated stars, but that maybe in my past life, I lived here in Italy. Perhaps I was a vintner, or the wife of one and every morning I would wake to the sound of the countryside. And then go into town for necessities. And not care about the rest of the world. But then, when I think about it, it would be how I imagine it as me. As a different woman; life would be that woman's life. Perhaps she would have a yearning to see more of the world, how other people live.*

*Oh, too much to think about.*
*On to packing.*
*Love,*
*Mom*

***

The taxi driver put Risa's suitcase and handbag into the trunk of the car. Risa turned to Bertie, tears forming at the edge of her eyes.

"Well, this is it."

The women hugged. Risa saw tears in Bertie's eyes as well. Bertie said, "You will be fine. You are strong!"

Risa said, through a clogged throat. "But I'll miss you, Bertie."

"You must go now; you don't want to miss your flight!"

"True. Okay."

They held each other at arms' length. Bertie let go first. She looked at the driver, who was standing with one foot halfway into the car. She waggled a finger at him. "Stai attento ora!"

The driver nodded and said, "Ok, I will. Sei pronto adesso?"

Bertie said, "She is ready now."

Risa got into the cab, and they drove off. She took one last glimpse of the Inn as the driver made a quick U-turn, then she turned to face forward.

She pulled the slightly worn cream colored card from her purse where it was nestled in a small compartment right next to the velvet trinket bag. She held it in the palm of her hand, closing her eyes, feeling the energy from it.

***If light is in your heart, you will find your way home.***

## CHAPTER FORTY-FIVE

*Boston Logan Airport*
*International Arrivals*
*May 28, 1982*

During the long flight from Rome, Risa tried to get some sleep but was restless. It was not the canopy bed at the Inn, or the gentle breezes coming in through the windows. The activity on the flight was constant, a baby was colicky up a few rows at the bulkhead, there was turbulence over the Atlantic. The food was just so-so.

She saw him first. He did not recognize her, as his eyes scanned right by her to the arriving passengers. At first she was dismayed but then remembered, her entire look was different.

But as she walked closer to him, he looked at her, his eyes widened, then he smiled and ran toward her, throwing his arms around her and picking her up off the floor. She held him around the shoulders and nuzzled her face into his neck. He smelled so good, like home, yet so foreign.

He set her back down. "My God, let me look at you!"

She held his arms. "You like?"

"My God!" he said again. "You are just even more beautiful, although I don't know how that's possible! You glow!"

They kissed then embraced once again. He murmured, "Oh, how I missed you, Reese."

"I missed you too."

"Let's get you out of here and home. You must be exhausted."

"I am. A hot shower and some decent food would be perfect." They walked arm in arm in the throng of passengers to the baggage claim area.

Saul beamed as he stole glances at her. "I still can't get over the change, Reese."

While Risa reveled in the attention from her husband, she

experienced a momentary panic, fighting the urge to get on the next flight back to Italy, to the safety and kindness of Bertie Giancarlo. But she was home now. She was with her husband and would work hard on connecting with her daughter. She would sit around the dinner table with her parents and kin and talk and laugh about her travels. She would meet Peg for lunch and talk about the fabulous food, wine and people that was Italy. She would meet with Alice and share her experiences and give her the beautiful frame. She would reconnect with CAP.

But what she would not do was enter her son's bedroom. Not yet.

## CHAPTER FORTY-SIX

*The office of Alice Stern*
*Salem, MA*
*Wednesday June 9, 1982*

Alice opened the wrapped gift. When she saw what it was, she set it down on her lap and looked at Risa, slowly shaking her head. "This is just beautiful. You didn't have to—"

Risa cut her off, "But I did. When I saw the frame, I saw Amy's beautiful smiling face inside of it. She should be right there, on your desk, so you can see her every minute of every day."

Alice looked down at the frame again. "I just don't know what to say."

"Your smile says it all. Consider this a small token of my appreciation for you. You literally changed my life with an empty journal, which I might say is full and I've started on another one."

Alice smiled, "You have?" She reached out to set the frame on her desk then picked up her pad and pen. "I hope you'll share?"

"I will. But there is so much, and I don't even know where to start."

"How about we start with your re-entry to your life here?"

Risa nodded. "Well, it was bittersweet, to say the least. For a moment at the airport, I wanted to run back to Italy on the next flight. But then I felt Saul's arms around me, got lost in his scent, and knew I had to keep walking forward."

Alice nodded as she wrote her notes.

"The house, well, that's a different story." She shrugged her shoulders. "Of course, I wanted to get settled again but that first day I wasn't sure where to go, what to do. The house was clean, there was food in the fridge. Everything was almost as I left it. I walked around in a bit of daze, not to mention the time change. It took me a few days to recalibrate."

"You said the house was almost as you left it. What do you mean?"

"Saul and Rachel had gone to New York to pick up Corey's things. The boxes were neatly stacked, as is Saul's way of arranging things, not in the basement but in the garage. When I went to get in my car I felt an invisible tug to look at the boxes. I fought the tug and avoided them. But I know I am going to have to unpack them someday. I'm not sure how comfortable I am with them there—a little like an in-your-face reminder.

"Do you think maybe the sooner you get to them, the better it would be? As we've experienced in the past, the out of sight out of mind thing can backfire."

Risa asked, "Do you mind me asking what you did? I mean with Amy's things?"

Alice nodded and sighed, "It was, well, it was hell, Risa. Neither my husband nor I could go into her room for many months. My sons had not been born yet so we had to focus on moving. We finally ventured in when it was time to box up the house and leave. Going into her room brought it all back. We donated all her clothes and kept just a few things of hers to keep her with us, if you know what I mean."

"Oh, I do." She thought about PegLeg and the marble. She would keep those for the rest of her life.

Alice refocused the conversation. "So, tell me, how was it seeing Rachel?"

Risa shook her head. "It was…I don't know. She was cordial, commented on my new look, said I looked very Ingenue, asked if I'd had a good time. Seemed to like the leather jacket I bought for her. It fit her perfectly."

"Okay. I suppose that is better than nothing at all."

"Well, I asked her to go to Maine with me this coming weekend. She hemmed and hawed. I think her father had a private conversation with her. She agreed but it wasn't anything near what I'd hoped it would be."

"You were hoping she would be excited? Interested?"

"Of course, I did but…I think she agreed out of a sense of duty."

"What do you hope to accomplish with her?" Alice asked.

Risa thought about it for a moment. "To bridge a gap. I have some apologies to make."

"What kind of apologies?"

Risa fidgeted with her blouse hem. "I just owe her. As you know, our relationship was very different from mine and Corey's."

"Okay, would you like to share it with me?"

"Not yet. Let me see how the weekend goes and I'll let you know."

"Fair enough. So, tell me, how was your trip?"

Risa took in a breath then let it out slowly, running her hand over the cover of her journal. "I suppose it would be best if I said it was hard as hell yet amazing at the same time?"

"Okay. Where would you like to start?"

"I think I'd like to tell you about a perfect stranger."

"Okay."

"Her name is Bertella Giancarlo. She is the innkeeper at the Inn Firenze, where I stayed in Florence." Risa sat back into the folds of couch. "She was there at the precise moment, witnessed something most people would run from, and nursed me back to myself without batting an eye."

Alice wrote quickly. "And?"

"And, well, Bertie—as she likes to be called—saved my life."

Alice leaned in, "Saved your life?"

"I lost it, Alice. I lost it in that little room thousands of miles away from home. I experienced something I've never experienced before, and God help me hope to never experience again. I went into a fury; I thought I was going to lose my mind. It felt like, well, like a volcano. Simmering at first, then without warning a blistering..." she searched for words, "emotional eruption that terrified me. So deep and so foreign. Does this sound normal?"

Alice sat back now, nodding. "Yes, it does. I was wondering when that would happen."

The women sat in silence for a few moments. Risa asked, "What do you mean, you were wondering when that would happen?"

"It was there. Lurking in the ethers, as we like to say. As your therapist, it is my job to not only listen to you; ask questions, probe, and take notes; but to stay one step ahead of you if possible. You've undergone a tremendous loss. Your life was upended. It was bound to happen."

"I suppose so."

"So, this perfect stranger was there at the precise moment for you?"

"Yes, she was. I had no control. I really, *really* lost it, Alice. I've never been so scared of what was inside me. It was like a monster on a runaway train. I had no control…" she looked away from Alice, afraid she might cry.

Alice's voice was gentle. "It is frightening. I know. Was there something that triggered it?"

"Yes. I saw a Corey look-alike at a café the first day I was there. It wasn't something you and I even thought to prepare for. He even moved like him. His smile…" She grabbed a tissue from the box. "Damn it," she allowed the tears to run.

Alice waited for Risa to regain her composure. She said, "Yes, you are right. We passed right over that possibility. I am sorry, Risa."

"Don't be sorry. It happened the way it was supposed to. Both Bertie and I agreed that it was the right time, do you know what I mean?"

"Oh, yes, I know what you mean."

"I almost called you, but I knew deep down inside I had to weather the storm on my own. And for what it was worth, Bertie was there. Not Saul, not you, not anyone I knew."

"Sometimes emotion with a perfect stranger is the only way to feel safe. There are no expectations, nothing to hold you back."

"Except extreme embarrassment." Risa added wryly.

"Yes, there is that. But sometimes the monster is too impatient and out it must come."

"Yes. It was a monster indeed."

Alice shifted in her chair. "Mind if we go off course for a moment?"

"No, please. You always come around anyhow."

Alice began, "Grief is a huge monster. Anything which changes our lives from what we deem normal to something chaotic reconstructs the architecture of how we perceive ourselves in our so-called normal life. Are you following me?"

"Sort of."

Alice continued, sitting forward now. "Think of it this way. You go along in life, and everything is doable—family, work, the weather, on and on. Something drastic happens and the body's involuntary fight or flight reaction takes over. So, when you first found out about Corey's sexuality and then all the way up until his last breath, you fought. You fought hard, Risa. Everything else in your life went onto the back burner. Nothing was going to come between a mother's love in survival mode for her child. Not even death. But in the end, death won out. You realized, painfully, that you were not included in the most important part of his life, and we will never really know why. So, at that point, right at that very point, your life took an entirely different route. And to add insult to injury, you were forced to keep it a secret from your family and friends. It was a completely unexpected diversion in your seemingly perfect life."

"Seemingly perfect life." Risa repeated mirthlessly. "I understand what you are saying now. The monster was building."

"Yes, devouring your energies, feeding on everything you knew to be the right way of life."

Risa wordlessly nodded her head. The conversation was beginning to envelope her, she felt like she was slowly sinking under water. She spoke aimlessly, quietly. "I will never know, will I?"

Alice asked gently. "Would you like to take a break?"

"No. Keep going." She continued to look off, anywhere but at Alice.

"This is tough stuff, Risa. I'm proud of you. You're going to be alright. You've already met the monster and begun your journey to recovery."

"Okay. Keep talking to me. I feel unsteady." She sat forward and gripped the edge of the low table in front of her.

Alice moved to the edge of her chair, focused on Risa's

reactions. "Stay with me. The beast has reared its ugly head and there are other things we must unearth to make sure it does not return. And this, Risa, will take time. This is where the real therapy begins. You are, finally, crawling out of the disaster; the monster named denial."

Risa repeated the word, "Denial." Then said, "Blindsided." She then looked Alice square in the eye. "Was I blindsided by my own denial? That the monster was really…me?"

Alice lifted her chin and nodded slowly. "Partly, yes."

Risa was now agape. With her heart thumping and her stomach churning, she felt the desire to crumble again. "My God," she whispered. Then more loudly, "My God."

***

Alice would not let Risa leave until she was sure Risa was on steady footing. After writing progress notes, she looked at the frame and smiled. She opened her desk drawer and withdrew the picture of Amy.

"There you are. You're going to have a new home! Such a beautiful frame for such a beautiful girl. Let's get you settled in, shall we?" She unlocked the back of the old frame and took out the photograph. Once inside the new frame, she cleared an area on her desk to accommodate Amy. "Yes, let's keep you right here. Right where you belong." Then said, "I think our Risa is going to make it. Now she must confront yet another demon, the relationship with her daughter. But this time, she has a few more tools to fight the monster. Let's pray she can stand firm even though she will feel like crumbling again.

## CHAPTER FORTY-SEVEN

Risa tried to be upbeat as she packed her small travel case for the weekend with Rachel. Something tugged at her soul, so she reread something she wrote in her journal which Alice repeated for her to write down:

*Just let yourself be. You will not be able to control the situation by avoiding it. Listen to her, let her speak. And if she chooses not to speak, you must be okay with that too. Remember, there are a lot of years that this has had to develop. If you should happen to crack it open, then you've made great progress. Be there for her. And you. This is about both of you. Take it slow.*

Risa had to check her desire to overcompensate. She wanted—needed— this situation to be resolved. And quickly. *But* she reasoned as she zipped up the case, *this is not who I am anymore, right? God. Who knows.*

They left the house in the late morning. Rachel insisted on listening to her own music on her Walkman with headphones on. Risa felt a gnawing tug at how disengaged Rachel was as her dissatisfaction with the whole thing was palpable. The drive north along the coast, while picturesque, was spent in non-companionable silence. Risa fought the desire to reach out to Rachel, to start a conversation of banalities. But every time she looked over, Rachel's eyes were closed with her body flattened against the passenger side door. It made Risa uncomfortable, tugged at her sore spots, anger, and rejection at the same time.

When they pulled into Ogunquit, Maine a few hours later, the afternoon sun was glistening off the current in the Atlantic and the town was awash in an easy, weekday groove.

Risa tried to lighten the mood when Rachel finally took off her headphones and clicked the Walkman off. "Your father and I used to come here all the time when we were dating."

Rachel shook her head. "Wow, mom. It's so easy for you to be happy." She looked out the window then mumbled, "Fake happy."

Risa looked at her daughter while stopped at a light. "I'm just reminiscing is all. You don't have to act so bothered by it. And what do you mean fake happy?"

Rachel shrugged and looked out the open window. "If you don't know by now, then."

Risa let it slide. She wasn't about to start the weekend off on the wrong foot, although from where she sat, it had been quite negative from the get-go.

Once at the Bed and Breakfast, Risa and Rachel got settled in and Risa suggested a café for lunch.

Rachel stood at the window, looking out at the ocean beyond the street below. "You know, Mom. I appreciate you taking the time to connect with me, but I'm not sure I can give you what you want."

Risa, thankful that her daughter at least opened the conversation, approached her gingerly, not wanting to force her to talk. "Thank you, honey. That's all I—"

Rachel turned toward her mother. "I agreed to come with you on this little," she made quotation marks with her fingers, "mother-daughter reunion because dad asked me to."

"He what?"

"He asked me to. He said it was important for me to bridge the gap with you before I went off to college."

"I think your dad is right. But I was hoping you'd be here, with me, out of a desire to truly bridge the gap and not just to say we did this thing together to appease your father."

"You sound like your therapist." Rachel sneered.

Risa shook her head slowly. "Rachel, really! Those are *my* words and *my* sentiments. I don't need a therapist to tell me how I feel about my own daughter!"

Rachel snorted and turned back to the view of the ocean. "Yeah."

"What *is* it, Rachel? What *is* it already?"

"It must have been nice for you to run away to Italy. Get away from us, from home. You even changed your look. Must have been lots of fun, huh Mom?"

Risa took a deep breath. "It was a very difficult trip, Rachel.

Perhaps later I can explain."

"Typical of you, not being present in the conversation."

"Rachel, I'm right here. What are you talking about?"

"About how you are."

"Which is?"

"Self-absorbed."

Risa sighed and sat down heavily on a loveseat. "Rachel..."

"Let me ask you something. Would we be having this conversation if Corey was still alive?"

Risa felt the sting of her words.

Rachel turned and said with emphasis, "See? You can't even answer me!"

Risa started, "It's not what you think! It's—"

Rachel cut her off. "It's *what*, then?" She started to pace the room. "You don't even know me."

"Now wait a minute, young lady!"

"No, if you want this to work between us, you have to listen to *me*."

Risa said, "I will listen. But I wish you would just sit down and talk calmly with—"

"What if I don't want to sit down, huh? What if I want to rant and rave or just walk all over the room, or just—"

Risa sat up straighter and watched as Rachel paced from one end of the room to the other until she stopped again at the window. Shades of her recent breakdown clouded her vision momentarily. She could only imagine what she looked like in that little room that fateful morning in Florence.

Rachel continued. "You're my mother. I didn't choose you, I'm a product of nature. I get that." She turned to face her. "But would I choose you if I had the choice? Probably not."

Risa's heart pounded in her chest. "*Rachel*, why are you being so hurtful?"

"Because, my whole life, Mother, my whole life I spent in Corey's shadow. If it weren't for dad..." she turned back to the view and muttered, "I don't know."

Risa hung her head. "My God. I never meant—"

"I know, you've told me this before."

Risa stood on shaky knees. She had never heard her

daughter speak with such vitriol. "What can I do? Tell me what I can do."

Rachel turned to her, tears running down her cheeks. "Ask me who I am. Learn about me the way you learned about Corey."

"I had four years to get to know Corey as a child and—"

Rachel finished the thought for her. "—And so, I guess when I came along you didn't have much energy left for me, right? Oh, sure, we went and did girlie things together occasionally. Clothes shopping—and believe me, some of the things you made me wear were *your* choices, not mine! Pedicures, manicures, facials. Do you know I couldn't care less what color my nails were or how perfect my toes looked in sandals? Or if my face was presentable from five miles away twenty-four-seven? I did it to appease *you*. To be the perfect, dutiful daughter!"

Risa sat back down on the couch, at a loss for words.

Mother and daughter remained in their own worlds for what felt like several minutes to Risa. Finally, Rachel broke the silence with her back still turned to her mother. "You know, Mom, Corey and I were close. He shared a lot of his life with me—the one he never shared with you and dad. He said he was petrified of what dad would do if he found out he was gay and was reluctant to let you down. You had such high hopes for him. He knew he couldn't fulfill your dreams. He knew you'd have been disappointed in him."

Risa shook her head, tears forming. She only wanted the best for her son. Ever.

Rachel continued, sniffling, and drying her eyes with the sleeves of her t-shirt. "Remember when I went to visit him that summer right before he got sick?"

"I do." Risa sniffed back a sob and reached into her purse for a tissue.

"He was living at Michael's—well, staying there mostly. He didn't want to come home. He was so happy. He said that Michael saved him."

"Saved him? From what?" She dabbed her eyes.

"Maybe I shouldn't be telling you this."

"Well, you started, why not continue?" She cleared her throat, swallowing hard.

"He got involved in things that would have killed you and dad."

Risa sat up straighter, "Like what?"

"Like the bars, the bath houses, the all-night parties."

"What do you mean, Rachel?"

At this she turned to face her mother. Leaning in, she spat, "The *bars*, mom. The *gay* bars! Where guys go to have *sex* with each other. Where they dress up in leather, and go around half-naked, and bed hop. Where they have sex in parks, in tunnels, behind trees, or right out in the open!"

Risa was aghast. "*What?*"

"There is a whole life you have no clue about, Mom, and he lived that life in New York City. While you and dad thought he was off studying, he was spending nights and sometimes days in a sexual stupor. He wrote it all down in a journal which he gave to me before he died. He made me promise to never show it to you."

"Where is this journal?"

Rachel sneered, "You can't read it."

Risa held herself at bay, barely. With her insides shuddering and her voice right on the edge, she said through gritted teeth, "You're right. I do not know you. *Not* at all." She turned on her heel and walked into the bedroom.

This was not going as planned. *Not* at all.

Risa sat on the edge of bed, her heart pounding. She had to collect herself before re-approaching her daughter. She had to take the high road or else they would get nowhere.

When she heard rustling from the living room and then the sound of the outer door closing, she got up quickly and found Rachel gone. There was a sealed envelope on the desk addressed 'Mom'.

"Oh, shit," Risa muttered, thinking her daughter had left her a goodbye note and was going to find her own way back to Boston. But when Risa looked out the big picture window to the ocean below, she saw that Rachel was walking on the beach toward a jetty. The tide was low. The rocks reached out to calm, lapping waves.

"Thank God." She reached for the envelope and opened it slowly, not sure what she would find inside.

*Mom*
*It's three AM and I can't sleep. So much I need to explain. Things you cannot imagine. Things that would never fit into your world of perfection. This place with all its constant lights and noise, where the night hides lust in the shadows. How do I explain all this when I am lost at sea without a beacon to guide me home? But you. You are strong! You will find your way home.*
*I am so sorry.*
*Please forgive me.*
*I love you,*
*C-*

"Oh, my God!" The shock of seeing something Corey had written to her coupled with the harsh exchange with Rachel finally took its toll. Tears ran hot down her cheeks. She pulled the card close to her chest, crossing her arms over it as if hugging him. "My baby. Oh, my baby. We failed you, didn't we?"

Swiping away her tears, she sat down on the couch and re-read his words. For a moment, feeling his presence in the room.

Then she realized a clarity she had not felt before this moment; it was *she* who asked Corey to *not* bring home his other life; it was *she* who closed the door! *She* was the one who silenced him. If *only* she had— "Damn it!" She stood up quickly, grabbed some tissues, her sunglasses, the room key, and with card in hand, jogged down to the jetty to join her daughter. She hoped it wasn't too late.

Risa sat down on a smooth rock just behind her daughter.

"Rachel."

"What, Mom."

"When was this written?"

"A week before he died. He couldn't hold on to the pen. I wrote it for him."

She asked, "Why did you wait so long to give it to me?"

"I wasn't going to, actually, give it to you."

Risa asked, "Why?"

Rachel did not answer.

Risa wanted to wrap her arms around her daughter's shoulders, but something held her back. "This must have been very difficult for you to write, let alone hang on to for so long."

Rachel's shoulders sagged. "He said I should use my judgment. Whether to give it to you or not. I didn't think you…"

Risa waited for a few moments then asked, "You didn't think I what, Rachel?"

She said in a small, quiet voice, "Deserved it."

Risa hung her head, feeling the chasm between them. She was heartbroken, but in a different way; Rachel was alive, and here, and there was still time to close the gap. She asked, "So, what made you change your mind?"

"I don't know. I thought maybe now was the right time."

"How so?"

"Because you're not as fragile as you were after he died. Maybe you're stronger now. I don't know. Maybe I just wanted to…" Rachel's words trailed off.

Risa finished the sentence for her. "Hurt me? Maybe because of all the hurt I caused you?"

Rachel started to cry. "Maybe."

Risa acted on her urge and gently took Rachel by her shoulders. When Rachel didn't turn away, she reached around and held her from behind. "I understand, Rachel. I really think I do. I am truly sorry. For so many things. Things I cannot, obviously, make up for at this moment. I am so sorry for your pain, that I wasn't there for you."

Rachel cried. "I miss him so much. And I miss you."

Risa felt her tears rise again. She leaned her head on Rachel's back. "I know, honey. I miss you, too."

"And…he, well, he told me so many things. Things that he should have probably told you and Dad. Like…"

Risa waited a beat then asked, "Like?"

Rachel broke the hug and turned to face her mother. There was no longer any rancor in her voice. She said matter-of-factly, "Like how misunderstood he felt. How he *had* to live two lives.

How troubled he was about his sexual desires. He said he..."

"What, honey. What did he say?" She gave Rachel a tissue.

"He said he couldn't get enough of it."

Risa dried her eyes. "Enough of?"

"The lifestyle. It was like a drug for him. He knew he was handsome; knew he could lure any man. He seemed so, I don't know, thirsty for it, do you know what I mean?"

Risa held herself in check. "I think so. Do you think he was misunderstood because he wasn't honest?"

Rachel replied, "He wasn't honest because he was always in some kind of conflict with himself."

"Okay. I can understand that now." Amazed that Rachel had this simple awareness, and she did not.

"To you and Dad, and everyone else, he was this golden boy—the handsome, playful, charming, loving kid that no one could resist. People flocked to him; people loved being around him. But he didn't know who he was inside. And it took someone like Michael to ground him. He said it himself. He was not proud of who he was when no one was looking."

Risa nodded and looked out at a tanker on the horizon. It seemed to hang in the mid-afternoon glare of the sun. "I am learning, Rachel. This is all so new to me. I never imagined for a moment that Corey would do anything but lead a normal life."

"A normal life to you and Dad. He knew deep down inside that being gay *was his* normal."

Risa blurted, "I went to see Michael after Corey died."

Rachel hesitated for a moment then asked, "You did?"

"Yes. I wanted to see where Corey spent his time."

"Did you find what you were looking for?"

Risa sighed. "I found more pieces of the puzzle and truthfully, they made me very sad. It seemed like such a good place for Corey to be. Especially now that you've told me about his...other life."

Rachel rocked a little bit. "Mom, why did Dad hate gay people so much?"

Risa breathed out and thought for a moment. Was it her place to tell Rachel the truth or was it Saul's responsibility? She decided to answer her. "He had an unfortunate experience as a young boy with an uncle who took advantage of him."

"What? Really?"

"Yes."

"Oh, my God, mom!"

"And when his uncle showed more attention to him than he did to Steven, your dad believed it was what love was supposed to be…because there was so little of it from his parents. Until it became a perversion. And then, your father confused the perversion with the actual meaning of the word homosexual. To him, the whole thing was evil and disgusting. When his uncle was made to leave town, he watched the only person who showed him any real love abandon him."

"Oh, Dad…" She hung her head. "What an awful thing."

"Yes, so, I'm sure if you went to your dad to talk about it, he would tell you. He is not proud of it. Your dad was confused and hurt at the same time. You know, he carried that terrible secret around since he was young. I never knew about it until, well, until something unfortunate happened before Corey died."

"What happened?"

"Grandma Elaine saw Corey kissing Michael in the hospital room. She made a surprise visit."

Rachel's eyes widened. She shook her head slowly, "Oh, no!"

"Elaine came to the house—you weren't home that evening—and pretty much ambushed your father into telling me his dirty little secret—and chided us up one side and down the other about how we dared to keep Corey's life from them—how Grandpa Nate was going to be devastated. Kissing a man, and a black man to boot!"

Rachel tried unsuccessfully to stifle a laugh. "Oh, to be a fly on the wall for *that* one!"

Risa couldn't help but join her daughter, "Honey, you can't make this shit up!"

Rachel cackled and pointed to her mother, "Mom! I'm so proud of you! Finally!"

"Oh, honey, I'm not the prude you think I am."

Rachel shook her head. "Could have fooled me!"

Risa took Rachel's hands in hers. "I forgot what your

laughter sounds like. It's beautiful, honey. I've missed it so."

Rachel responded by holding her mother's hands a little tighter. She asked, "Are you proud of me?"

"Oh, my God! I couldn't be prouder! You are as smart as you are beautiful. You've always had a good head on your shoulders. Do you want to know something?"

"What's that?"

"I've always admired you. You will succeed at anything you put your mind to. You have this sense of order, just like your dad. You walked and talked before your brother, you tried and tried things until you got them right. You never gave up, Rachel. You're not a quitter. So many kids today are. But not you. Ruthie always said you'd probably be the first woman president of the United States!"

Rachel nodded. "I know. She tells me that all the time."

"Well, president or not, you will do good things in your life."

"Thank you, Mom. Really. Thank you." She smiled. "And I'm so excited about Harvard."

Risa smiled back at her. "We are too." She stumbled over her next words at first as a lump traveled up her throat, but when she swallowed and tried again, she said, "I love you so, Rachel. You are a stronghold in *my* life, and I am truly sorry for not being more present in *your* life." Tears ran down anyhow. "Oh, for heaven's sake, look at me, always crying."

Rachel pulled her mother in closer and held her. She too choked on a sob. "Well, at least you're back on this planet now. I was worried about you."

Risa started to laugh through her tears. "Oh, you."

They sat like that, unwilling to break free from each other until Rachel murmured into her mother's shoulder, "People will talk. They'll think we're lesbians or something."

Risa barked a guffaw. "Just let 'em!" She pulled her in closer. A surge of love emerged from the bottom of her soul and out of her arms. To Risa, the embrace was a place to restart and change the climate of their relationship. At that moment she was not willing to lose their precious connection because of society's demands of what was normal and what was not.

She was finally and unequivocally tired of society.
She repeated, "Just let 'em."

## CHAPTER FORTY-EIGHT

*The Office of Alice Stern*
*June 15, 1982*

Risa shared Corey's note with Alice.
"That is just beautiful. How does it make you feel?"
Risa thought for a moment then said, "You know, Alice. Bittersweet. Suffice it to say that it was a turning point for me. Things happen when they are supposed to, right?"
Alice smiled and nodded. "You're catching on. I'm proud of you, Risa."
Risa said, "You know, there *is* a part of me that wants to read his journal."
"And the other part?"
"Knows it's something sacred. But somehow, I feel a lot of the answers I've been looking for are between those pages."
Alice nodded, "That could very well be. Do you think it's a good idea to read this right now. Or ever, for that matter."
"Maybe it will help me move on?" Risa questioned.
"Perhaps but let me digress for a moment. How would you feel if someone were to read your private journal?"
Risa thought about it then said, "I think it would depend upon who I wanted to share it with, if anyone."
"So, would it stand to reason that Corey shared his journal with Rachel because they were, I don't know, closer in age? She did not pose a threat?"
"You have a point." She shifted her position on the couch and crossed her legs. "Maybe."
"Do you think Corey trusted her with his inner-most feelings?"
Risa nodded, "Obviously."
Alice continued, "So, let's go back to your journal. The difference here is that you are still alive and can make a choice as to who you share it with. Corey shared it with Rachel so someone could know who he was since you and Saul were

unaware of this other life he lived."

Risa nodded again, her throat constricting.

Alice leaned forward and said gently, "Risa, is it more because he chose to not share this life with you or is it more about the words in that journal? The parts of him that you did not know. The parts that defined him."

Risa reached for a tissue. "This is very hard, Alice."

Alice said, "I know, Risa. I know."

Risa looked down at the tissue in her hand. "Why is the truth so hard to understand, to swallow?"

Alice waited to answer her.

She looked up, "I hate that he cut me out." Her words came out in a tearful sigh. "I thought he trusted me unconditionally…but that he had to *hide* who he was. It just breaks my heart that we made him feel that way. He was so lost…"

Alice nodded and set her pad to the side. "Perhaps he was not proud of the way he carried on his life. Perhaps he wanted to spare you more anguish and grief. We will never really know." She waited a beat then said, "I would say let it go."

Risa said, "I don't know if I can. I just really want to understand that part of him."

"I must ask. What do you hope to glean from this information? From everything we've discussed to date it sounds like he was caught up in a whirlwind of conflicting messages. Is that how you want to remember him?"

Risa looked down at her folded hands. "Of course not. But it was a part of him. A big part. It was who he was becoming, how he would have lived his life, had he lived."

Alice took a sip of water then said, "And perhaps it would have been different as you all evolved around his lifestyle, had he lived. It is ultimately your choice to read the journal or not. If you feel it would clear up some unanswered questions, to close the gap and help you to move on, then, read it."

"But you think I'd be making a mistake."

"I think it depends upon your perspective. I wonder if you might put it away for a later date. Give yourself some time to accept that he lived this other life without you."

Risa sighed deeply. "You're probably right. Maybe I just don't want to admit that."

"Maybe not now. But it will come, Risa."

Alice waited for a beat then switched gears. "So, it sounds like the trip with Rachel had a strong finish. I'm glad to hear that."

Risa was glad to change in subject. "Yes. Well, we're not in the clear yet but we can finally look each other in the eye and talk. She was hurt. I did not give her the life I gave Corey. I know that now and it's a big pill to swallow. We both realize that the extent of the damage is deep. I suppose it comes down to starting right now instead of trying to make up for years gone by."

Alice smiled, "I am proud of you both for forging ahead."

"Thank you."

Alice asked, "So, tell me. Have you thought about getting back on stage?"

"Yes, I have. My seat on the Board is still available. I'm going tomorrow to pick up some scripts for next year. I miss it terribly."

"I'm very happy to hear that, too." Alice set her pad and pen down, sat back and took off her glasses. "You ever think about writing a play? Or a book?"

Risa's eyebrows rose. "A book, play? About what?"

"Your experience with losing your son. The why's and how's but more importantly your journey through it."

Risa thought about it for a moment. "No. Well, that's not entirely accurate. When I was in Italy I thought about writing a one-woman show. I liked the idea of it but the actual execution of it. I'm not a writer."

"You don't have to be. That's what good copy editors are for."

"But who would want to read about my journey? I mean, really."

"Anyone who has lost a loved one to HIV, to conflict."

"But I'm no expert on it. It's just my feelings."

"It's those feelings, the ones near and dear to your heart that would capture other grieving hearts. It's not fiction, it's real. You could reach many."

Risa nodded but said nothing. She could not imagine putting her words on paper for others to read.
*But then again…*

\*\*\*

On her way home, she turned off the radio and said out loud, "Well, Core. What do you think? Is Alice on to something here? Maybe I *could* make a difference in someone else's life. Share the pain and grief so they know they are not alone. Maybe I *could* do that."

She played some ideas in her head and almost missed her exit off route 128. She decided to pull into a small market to pick up some fresh tomatoes, Buffalo mozzarella cheese, and basil. She would make an antipasto with olives and capers, fresh Italian bread sliced thin then grilled with olive oil, a la Bertie Giancarlo.

She wanted to make something special for her family; to sit with them, share a bottle of wine, and just 'be'.

Outside on the patio.

Into the twilight hours as the sun sets fire-like over the tops of distant trees, as stars start to emerge.

Just sit with Saul and Rachel and take in the beauty of their simple existence.

Yes, she would provide that for her family.

Something she had not done in a very, very long time.

"The reality is that you will grieve forever. You will not 'get over' the loss of a loved one, you will learn to live with it. You will heal and you will rebuild yourself around the loss you have suffered. You will be whole again but you will never be the same. Nor should you be the same nor would you want to."
--Elizabeth Kubler-Ross

*-and always-*

**If light is in your heart, you will find your way home.**
-Anonymous

# Letters to Corey

# EPILOGUE

**TEN YEARS LATER**
*The Boston Park Plaza Hotel*
*Grand Ballroom*
*Saturday November 2, 1991*

"Good evening and welcome to the annual gala dinner for the National AIDS Coalition! It is my pleasure to introduce our keynote speaker tonight. She is an author, actor, activist, but foremost a mother. When she lost her son to HIV in nineteen eighty-one, she forged the journey from loss to surrender. Like many of you here tonight, she has given her loss a purpose. You've read about her experiences in her book *Letters to Corey*, you've seen her on the Oprah Winfrey Show, listened to her on NPR, and attended the many plays she has performed right here in our time-honored Boston theatre district! Tonight, we present her with the award of excellence. Please welcome to the podium the president of the New England Chapter of the National AIDS Coalition, Mrs. Risa Shapiro."

Risa enters the stage to a standing ovation. When the crowd settles back down at their tables, she looks out at the sea of faces. She begins:

"Thank you. It is an honor to be here tonight, to accept this award. This would not be possible without the support of my strong, beautiful family." She takes a moment to smile down from the stage to the head table, where Saul, Rachel, Rachel's husband Jeffrey, Abe, Ruth, and Elaine and Nathan sit. "Two days ago, would have been my son's thirtieth birthday."

The customary response throughout the Coalition when there was a birthday or death-date announced was to lightly tap a knife or spoon on glassware to signify solidarity. Risa waited until the clinking died down then continued.

"We always used to kid him about being a trick or a treat. Most often, he was a treat." She smiles warmly. "The tradition in our family is to gather together to celebrate Corey's birthday at various venues. This last one was actually very quiet at his gravesite. It was just my husband and my daughter and me. We each decided to write a personal message for him then leave the messages in a small metal box which we set next to his stone. It was bittersweet to say the least. You see, the thing about grieving is that it never really goes away. We accept the loss and weave it into the fabric of our daily life. We've come such a long way, all of us in this room who have lost someone. We smile, we laugh, we forge on. But we never forget. We don't fill that gap. We know it is unfillable. It's been a long road for me, for my family. There were days, months when I wasn't sure who I was anymore, only to find the real me hidden beneath layers of denial, bitterness, grief, anger, and most of all fear. Fear of the unknown. Fear that the new normal might be evasive at best! No one should have to travel this road alone! And we can be there for others who feel isolated or frightened of what the future might hold for them, for their family. The Coalition sees to that as much as we can. But we need more voices! Your voices!"

She takes a moment, during the applause, to sip water from a glass that had been pre-set for her. "When my husband and I decided to move out of our house on Cape Ann to Boston, it was the next logical step in changing the landscape. When Saul shifted his practice from corporate law to defending discrimination cases, he found a challenging and productive path which not only makes him feel closer to Corey but to others like Corey who continue to struggle with loss of jobs, expulsion from school, or defamation on *any* level. And I found that my own path finally had meaning and direction. Why, I remember when I first started out with the Coalition when I still lived on the Cape; speaking to nearly empty rooms, I was discouraged but was reassured by the powers that be that once the fire was lit, it would flourish. And, as you can see, it did. But no one wanted to hear about HIV or admit to it. It was taboo, hush-hush. Society—at least where we lived—wasn't ready for it. Then, women started to trickle in from other counties. It was more of a therapeutic type of circle where we talked about the enormity of the pain of loss, the gravity of the situation, the secrecy and familial scorn about being gay. Soon, men joined us, men who had lost partners, their friends who had lost friends, and the list became much longer. Then we realized we needed a larger space. Instead of twice a month, the meetings became weekly. We moved the operation to Swampscott, where the good people at the Inn on the Bay gave us use of one of their conference rooms for a nominal fee. It was the generosity of business owners that helped propel the Chapter into what it has become today. On the local level, let's thank Nancy Grant of Nancy's Sweet Treats who continues to supply pastries and coffee, Vittorio's pizzeria who brings in fresh hot pies and incredible Italian fare, George the video technician who helps us with visual materials and who is, actually, manning all the technical shows you are seeing tonight, and Eagle Printing who, on several last-minute jobs, supplied us with all the written materials. Please give them a round of applause."

She takes another sip of water while the audience responds, then continues. "Four years later, here we are, one of the strongest chapters in the country—next to the west coast, of course. The National Coalition is gathering strength in the Midwest, the South, and now we are reaching into Canada. Your contributions make the outreach that much stronger. And I would be remiss if I did not thank Oprah Winfrey and her very generous donations on a yearly basis. Between her sponsorship and outreach, the Coalition has moved to the forefront of the public eye. She is a true humanitarian."

She dons reading glasses and picks up a sheaf of papers. "I draw your attention to the yearly report. Our financials prove the indisputable support for families and individuals who otherwise would not be able to afford critical medical interventions. The funds have increased exponentially over the years; saving hundreds of families and individuals who would otherwise have been left behind or worse. The research component of the report clearly demonstrates how our dollars are at work in the laboratories and facilities that depend on early detection of the virus. Also, our funds range from home health care to education and prevention. I won't bore you with the numbers, you can certainly read those yourselves."

She sets the papers down and removes her glasses. "But

what I will say is this. It takes heart to be here, to believe in something that supports the greater good of our communities. Each and every one of you has a voice, and the more you share that voice, the wider the circle becomes. Yes, it is about money, about research, about education, about finding a way to slow the spread of this insidious virus once it attacks the body. It's not just the gay plague anymore. In fact, it never really was. It's not about secrecy—we must *all* be open to the truth! Denial is a roadblock! And, you know what, let's *not* leave the nay-sayers and detractors behind, instead let's *educate* them, *invite* them to march strong with our solidarity. We owe it to the loved ones we lost and to the ones who are losing the battle right now, today. HIV-AIDS is *not* going away anytime soon. Educate, equip, keep moving forward with open hearts and eyes focused on the future!"

She nods during the applause. When it dies down, she states, "I thank you for bestowing this award to me however, I must share it with all of you who continue to work towards a future where HIV-AIDS will be something *not* to hide from or be ashamed of. Where infected individuals do not feel like they have been abandoned but are shown the care and respect they deserve. We can do this, my friends. We can help in geographical areas where the resources are slim, we must change the landscape of age-old societal constraints. *We cannot let society win with this one! We must be strong*!"

She lifts the award plaque and says, "Good night and thank you." Tears gather as the audience gives her a standing ovation. She nods into the spotlight, knowing Corey is smiling down at her.

Once offstage, she is given a brilliant, colorful bouquet of flowers. Saul is there to bring her into his arms. His face is wet from tears, too. He whispers into her ear, "I am so proud of you, Reese. You've come such a long way. We are *all* so very proud." He kisses her and then they are ushered to another area of the ballroom for photographs of her family and the national officers from the Coalition.

It is a night she will never forget.

An accolade she owes to Corey and her entire family.

And to Alice, Bertie, and to an elderly wise man in Tuscany with yellowed fingernails.

*October 31, 1991*
*Happy birthday son,*
*My heart continues to fill with pride. Your name is always just a breath away, always on the periphery of my being.*

*Over the years, I've come to understand that your death was not only your journey but all of ours.*

*In therapy, Alice helped me to understand many things, things that took me years to fully grasp.*

*She taught me that as mothers, we have an innate duty to give our children the best that we can with what we've got. And at the time I thought I was doing a yeoman's job of raising the perfect child. But then that world started to fracture, you went a different way, something I could not control. Something I inadvertently excised myself from, something I could not face. So, I drew the line between us, and you led your life the way you saw fit, and I closed my eyes. And in your very young, impressionable years, you did just that, all the while convincing us, me, that you were still the same Corey. And you were, only, I didn't understand how the two of you—the one I always thought you were and the one you were becoming— connected until it was too late.*

*Being in therapy while you were alive kept me focused. Therapy after you died was my unraveling. I fought it, I rallied and kept beating the monster back with denial. After Italy, a fissure erupted and then I found myself on a long painful journey toward surrender.*

*The first thing I had to learn after you died was how to talk to you—which thankfully came in the form of a journal. And the second was and continues to be making peace with the fact that I lost the opportunity to apologize to you, to explain. Face to face. It was a slow process of admission, Corey. And I am fallible, faltering from time to time. And when that happens, I look to our family—because really, that is all we truly have.*

*As my relationship with Rachel continues to emerge, and as I watch her with her own children, I feel I've been given another* chance. Rachel maintains that so many things could have changed the outcome of our lives, yet those things did not happen because they weren't supposed to. This was to be our fate. I believe that now. I have learned how to beat back the darkness and not let it shade the beauty of my grandchildren's lives, no matter what they become.

Another integral piece of the puzzle revealed in therapy was the reason why I exposed you to everything I could from the time you were born; to make every life moment count. I wanted to fill you to the brim! I wanted you to have it all! Because I now know this, Corey. On that cold night in February, when you were four months old and I held you in my arms, I knew I was going to lose you. So, I kept you close, took your hand, and guided you.

But then, you grew into early manhood and let go of my hand to take the reins into the life that was rightfully yours, where I was no longer your guide.

Until the end.

Again.

When I held both your hands as you took your last breath.

Son, today and every day I am blessed with people in my life who complete the ever-shifting puzzle. And what we all know is this: We are all flawed, looking for answers to difficult questions, each in our own worlds. Having navigated the darkness of pain and loss without a compass, lost in a sea of blinding truths—I see what Alice meant when she said that we are all warriors on this road to humanity.

I am convinced we survive only one way: with unconditional love. And from that unconditional love grows respect, understanding, and acceptance.

And even through the separateness, we join hands to create a strength that knows no bounds.

We are the living strongholds of our frames!

So here are our letters to you, in this metal box.

You continue to be a mitzvah in our lives.

I love you,

Mom

Risa folds her letter, lays it into the box with the others, then gently lowers the lid and engages the latch. She leaves a customary handful of stones on the top of his headstone then nestles the box snug to the flowers that surround the bottom of the granite.

When she rises, she kisses her fingertips to his engraved name, then breathes deep the glorious New England Fall air, joining her husband and her daughter in the car.

## *-The End-*

# Letters to Corey

## ACKNOWLEDGEMENTS:

Writing is a singular art, but it takes a village to get it off the ground. Since its inception five years ago, *Letters to Corey* has taken four iterations. During that time several people read it, commented on it, and then I shelved it for a year because the story was all over the place and unfocused.

Then, one night in early spring of this year while prepping dinner in the kitchen, a thought came into my head, and I said out loud—this to the dogs who were lined up behind me patiently waiting for a few morsels to zing their way— "It's time."

That was seven months ago.

So please allow me to thank the front line:

**Tracy Reuss**—The one who listened with objective ears and pointed out the connects and disconnects in the flow of the arc, who cried at all the right places and said, "You got this." Thank you, thank you.

**Our Five Foster Fails**—Dangerous Dottie, Maizie, Cass, Silas, Owen, and Luce-the-cat. Our hearts still beat for the ones we lost in 2023: Stew and Cooper.

**The Bitchfest Ladies** from the beautiful lands near Charlevoix, Michigan—Barb, Kate, Nancy, Diane, Noreen and Frankie, and any stragglers who happened in during a reading in Diane's living room. Early beta readers.

**The Ladies of Harley**—Whose steady support for my creative endeavors is unwavering.

**Bonnie Moakley**—Beta read, line edits, continuity, also a LOH member.

**Meryl Graham**—Copy Editor

**Randy Lake**—Artistic Director at Great Escape Stage Company in Marshall, Michigan.

**Laura Henderson-Whiteford**—Of SHE Films Media.

**Rabbi Lawrence Kushner**—For his beautiful words.

**Joe Bulko**—My favorite theologian. So many great talks, look forward to many more.

**Steve Bennett**— CEO of Authorbytes.

**Barb Vanderwheele,** RNFA—Medical Advisor.

**Ann McMan--** Cover Art.

**Karen Badger**—Format and Cover Editor

**To you, the reader.**

# **BOOK CLUB DISCUSSION**

1. What did you think about Risa's omission of the truth about her son to her husband?

2. Did you think Risa was more concerned about her and her family's reputation rather than how difficult it may have been for Corey to admit his sexuality to himself, let alone others?

3. Risa has her psychotic break with a stranger. Do you think it's easier to be vulnerable with someone you do not know?

4. Do you agree with Rabbi Lawrence Kushner that we are all pieces of a puzzle and come into one another's life for a specific purpose?

# Letters to Corey

## ABOUT THE AUTHOR

Ellen Bennett lives in southwest Michigan with Tracy, their five foster fail dogs, and one elderly feline. Ellen is the author of the Pagodaville series (the play form is on its second iteration with hopes of production in 2025-2026). She has published several short stories in on-line forums and is a community actor, hiker, motorcycle enthusiast, fabulous dog mom, and avid reader. Look for the audio version of *Letters to Corey* to be released sometime later this year.

Thank you for reading this book. Please feel free to leave a comment on Amazon or Goodreads. Your honesty is appreciated.

Find us on Facebook and Instagram at Cojinito Press, LLC or contact us at cojinitopressllc@gmail.com.

Made in the USA
Middletown, DE
23 January 2024